Ultimate Fondue Rec

Over 150 Recipes
to Master the Art of Fondue
from Traditional to Innovative

MW00899136

Otes Sartre

Table of Content

Introduction

Welcome to the delicious world of fondue, where every dip and swirl in a communal pot invites connection, conversation, and culinary creativity. Fondue, a dish beloved around the globe, offers more than just a meal; it presents an experience, a way to gather friends and family around a single pot of melting delight that promises warmth and joy.

In this journey through the art of fondue, we aim to rekindle the timeless charm of this communal eating tradition while exploring both its classic roots and the innovative twists that can transform simple ingredients into a feast. Whether you are a novice eager to set up your first fondue pot or a seasoned enthusiast looking to push the boundaries of flavor, this guide is designed to equip you with all you need to master the art of fondue.

Fondue has a storied history, originating from the Swiss Alps as a means for villagers to use aged cheeses and stale bread during the harsh winter months. From these humble beginnings, it has evolved into a sophisticated, versatile dish that spans various cultures and ingredients. The beauty of fondue lies not just in its rich flavors but in its ability to bring people together. It's about the shared moments as much as it is about the food. Every pot becomes a centerpiece, around which people gather to dip and share from a communal dish, creating an intimate bond.

In this guide, we delve deep into the essence of fondue. From the silky smoothness of cheese fondues to the sizzling delights of broth-based fondues, we explore the wide array of styles and ingredients that can cater to any palate. Through detailed discussions and expert tips, we provide a comprehensive look at how to select the right fondue pot, balance flavors, and choose the perfect accompaniments that enhance rather than overwhelm the fondue experience.

Moreover, we will introduce you to the tools and equipment that make fondue preparation not just easy but also enjoyable. Understanding these tools will elevate your fondue dishes and ensure that your dining experience is as smooth as the fondue itself.

Our guide is more than just a collection of recipes; it is a passage into a world of interactive dining that values the joy of eating together. It encourages you to experiment with flavors, learn new techniques, and embrace the communal spirit of fondue dining. As you turn each page, you will find yourself equipped to host a fondue party that will linger in the memories of your guests long after the last morsel is enjoyed.

So, gather your ingredients, invite your friends, and prepare to dip into the convivial world of fondue. Here, every meal is an adventure and every pot a promise of a shared experience that is as enriching as it is delicious.

Fondue Basics

Fondue is both an art and a culinary practice that centers around a communal pot, where guests dip bread, meats, vegetables, or fruits into a delicious, molten concoction. Whether it's the traditional cheese fondue, the hearty meat fondue cooked in oil or broth, or the sweet chocolate fondue, the basics of making a successful fondue are fundamentally about balance, flavor, and the right equipment. Here, we delve into the fundamental aspects of preparing fondue, ensuring each pot is a gateway to a delightful dining experience.

1. Understanding the Ingredients

The success of a fondue largely depends on the quality and type of ingredients used. For cheese fondue, the choice of cheese is crucial. Traditional recipes often blend different types such as Gruyère, Emmental, or Appenzeller. Each cheese offers a distinct flavor and melting characteristic that contributes to the fondue's overall texture and taste. When making chocolate fondue, opt for high-quality chocolate with a high cocoa content to ensure a smooth and rich result.

2. The Right Mix

For cheese fondue, the cheese must be melted with a liquid to achieve the right consistency. Dry white wine is a classic choice as it adds acidity which helps to balance the richness of the cheese and ensures a smooth melt. A splash of lemon juice can also help in keeping the cheese fondue from becoming stringy. For a non-alcoholic version, you can use lemon juice and milk as substitutes. In chocolate fondue, a small amount of cream or milk is essential to keep the chocolate flowing and glossy.

3. Preparing the Pot

The caquelon, or fondue pot, should be made of a material that conducts heat well and retains it, such as ceramic or enameled cast iron. Before adding your ingredients, rub the inside of the pot with a clove of garlic to infuse it with flavor. When making cheese fondue, first dissolve a little cornstarch in the wine to prevent the cheese from clumping and to achieve a smooth, creamy texture.

4. Heating Techniques

It's important to heat your fondue gently. Cheese and chocolate fondue should never be cooked on high heat as this can cause the cheese to seize or the chocolate to burn, leading to a gritty texture. Instead, melt the ingredients slowly and stir consistently. If using a stovetop, cook the fondue on low heat until the ingredients are melted and then transfer it to a fondue burner that maintains low, even heat.

5. Dippers and Accompaniments

The choice of dippers is essential in complementing the flavors of your fondue. For cheese fondue, pieces of crusty bread, blanched vegetables, apple slices, and boiled small potatoes work well. Meat fondues, cooked in hot oil or broth, are usually accompanied by sauces and dips alongside a variety of meats and vegetables. For chocolate fondue, fresh fruits like strawberries and bananas, marshmallows, pound cake, and biscotti are popular choices.

6. Tips for Success

- Always shred or cut cheese into small pieces for quicker and more even melting.
- Keep all ingredients at room temperature before starting to make the fondue to ensure even cooking.
- Stir the fondue in a figure-eight pattern to blend the ingredients smoothly and prevent burning at the bottom.
- Keep the fondue covered when not actively dipping to maintain the optimal temperature and consistency.

Mastering the basics of fondue making is not just about following recipes but also about understanding the interplay of ingredients, heat, and timing. With these fundamental tips, anyone can host a successful fondue gathering, delighting guests with the rich flavors and communal charm that fondue uniquely offers.

Setting Up Your Fondue Pot

Creating the perfect fondue experience begins with setting up your fondue pot correctly. This subchapter provides a detailed, step-by-step guide to preparing your fondue set for the first time, ensuring you have everything you need to enjoy this delightful dish without any hitches.

1. Choose the Right Fondue Pot

The type of fondue you plan to make determines the kind of pot you should use. For cheese and chocolate fondue, a ceramic or enameled cast iron pot is ideal because it distributes heat evenly and keeps the fondue warm without burning it. For meat fondue, where higher temperatures are needed for cooking meat in oil or broth, a metal pot, such as stainless steel or copper, is recommended because it can handle the heat without damaging the pot.

2. Assemble the Necessary Equipment

Before you start, make sure you have all the necessary equipment:

- **Fondue Pot**: As per your choice based on the type of fondue.
- **Burner**: Most fondue sets come with an alcohol, gel, or butane burner. Ensure it is filled with the appropriate fuel and functioning correctly.
- **Fondue Forks**: These are long forks used by each guest to dip the food into the pot. Each fork typically has a different colored handle to help guests keep track of their fork.
- **Stand or Base**: Provides a stable foundation for the pot and houses the burner.
- **Fuel:** The type of fuel depends on your burner type. Common options include butane, alcohol, or fondue gel.

3. Prepare the Pot

Before using your fondue pot for the first time, wash it with warm, soapy water to remove any residues from manufacturing. Rinse well and dry thoroughly. If you are using a ceramic or cast iron pot, you may want to season it by rubbing the inside with a garlic clove. This not only seasons the pot but also adds a subtle flavor to your fondue.

4. Set Up the Burner

Make sure your burner is ready to use. If you're using an alcohol or gel burner, fill it with the appropriate fuel, ensuring not to overfill. For butane burners, insert the butane cartridge according to the manufacturer's instructions. Test the burner to make sure it ignites properly and adjust the flame to the desired level. The flame should be steady but not too high to avoid scorching the fondue.

5. Arrange the Ingredients

Prepare all ingredients before heating the fondue. If making cheese fondue, grate or cube the cheese and mix it with any flour or cornstarch as needed. This helps in melting the cheese smoothly and preventing clumps. For chocolate fondue, chop the chocolate into small, even pieces to ensure it melts uniformly. If you are preparing meat fondue, cut the meat into bite-sized pieces, and prepare any broths or oils.

6. Heating Your Fondue

Once everything is prepared, place the pot on the burner. Add the initial ingredients (like wine or broth) and heat them gently. Once the liquid is warm, gradually add your main ingredients like cheese or chocolate, stirring consistently. For meat fondues, heat the oil or broth to the correct temperature before guests begin dipping.

7. Regulate the Heat

Adjust the flame as needed to keep the fondue at the ideal temperature. Cheese and chocolate fondues should be kept warm enough to stay melted and smooth, but not so hot as to burn. Meat fondues require a higher temperature to ensure the meat cooks properly.

8. Enjoy Your Fondue

Once everything is set and the fondue is heated, invite your guests to start dipping using their fondue forks. Remember, fondue is not just about eating; it's about the experience of sharing and enjoying the company.

By following these steps, you'll ensure that your fondue set is perfectly prepared for any gathering. Whether it's a cozy dinner for two or a festive party, a well-set fondue pot is the centerpiece of a memorable meal.

Choosing Your Ingredients

Selecting the right ingredients for your fondue is pivotal to crafting a dish that is not only delicious but also memorable. Whether you're planning a traditional cheese fondue, a decadent chocolate fondue, or a savory meat fondue, understanding how to choose the best cheeses, chocolates, broths, and oils will greatly enhance your fondue experience. This subchapter provides detailed guidance on making these selections to ensure every dip is delightful.

1. Selecting Cheeses for Fondue

The success of a cheese fondue largely hinges on the choice of cheese. A good fondue blend melts smoothly and offers a balanced flavor profile. Traditionally, Swiss cheeses like Gruyère and Emmental are preferred due to their creamy texture and rich flavor. However, you can also experiment with other varieties:

- Gruyère: Offers a slightly sweet yet earthy flavor, which melts beautifully.
- Emmental: Known for its smooth melting quality and a slightly nutty taste.
- Fontina: Provides a creamy texture and a mild, nutty flavor, excellent for melting.
- Comté or Beaufort: Adds a complex, slightly fruity flavor to the fondue.

For the best results, combine several cheeses to balance flavors and melting qualities. Ensure that the cheeses are grated or finely chopped to promote even melting. Avoid pre-shredded cheeses, as they often contain anti-caking agents that can affect the texture of the fondue.

2. Choosing Chocolate for Fondue

When it comes to chocolate fondue, the quality of the chocolate is key. High-quality chocolate will yield a smoother, more flavorful fondue:

- Dark Chocolate: Choose a high cocoa content (at least 70%) for a deep, rich flavor. Dark chocolate also melts well, making it ideal for fondue.
- Milk Chocolate: Provides a sweeter, creamier taste but can be a bit thick when melted. It's often best mixed with a bit of dark chocolate or thinned with cream.
- White Chocolate: Requires careful handling as it burns easily due to its high sugar and milk content. It offers a sweet, creamy flavor that pairs beautifully with fruits.

For chocolate fondue, chop the chocolate finely to ensure it melts evenly and mix with a small amount of cream to achieve a smooth consistency.

3. Selecting Broths and Oils for Meat Fondue

For meat fondue, also known as fondue bourguignonne, you can choose between cooking the meat in hot oil or in broth:

- Oils: Neutral oils like canola or peanut oil are preferred due to their high smoke points, which allow you to cook at higher temperatures without burning. These oils also have a mild flavor that doesn't overpower the meat.
- Broths: A flavorful broth can enhance the meat's flavor while being lighter than oil. Beef or chicken broth can be seasoned with herbs and spices for additional flavor. Vegetable broth is an excellent base for dipping vegetables alongside the meat.

Ensure the oil or broth is hot enough before starting to dip - typically around 375°F (190°C) for oil and simmering gently for broth.

4. General Tips for Choosing Ingredients

Freshness: Always opt for fresh and high-quality ingredients. Freshness affects both flavor and how well your ingredients will perform during cooking.

Local and Seasonal: Consider local and seasonal ingredients to ensure maximum flavor and freshness.

Experimentation: Don't hesitate to experiment with different combinations of cheeses or chocolates, or to infuse broths with unique flavors to suit your tastes.

Choosing the right ingredients is crucial for creating a fondue that is truly enjoyable. By focusing on quality and suitability for the specific type of fondue you're preparing, you can turn a simple meal into an extraordinary experience.

Tools and Equipment

A successful fondue party relies not just on great ingredients but also on having the right tools and equipment. This subchapter provides a comprehensive guide to the essential list of fondue equipment, ensuring you have everything needed to host a smooth and enjoyable fondue experience.

1. Fondue Pot (Caquelon)

The centerpiece of any fondue setup is the fondue pot, also known as a caquelon. The choice of pot depends on the type of fondue you plan to serve:

- **Ceramic Pots**: Best for cheese and chocolate fondue. Ceramic distributes heat slowly and evenly, preventing the fondue from burning.
- **Metal Pots**: Ideal for oil or broth fondues (meat fondue). Metal pots are better at handling the high temperatures needed for cooking meat.
- **Enamel-coated Cast Iron Pots**: Versatile for all types of fondue. They retain heat well and are suitable for cheese, chocolate, and meat fondues.

2. Fondue Burner

The burner heats the pot and keeps the fondue at the right temperature. There are several types of burners:

- Alcohol Burners: Commonly used with traditional fondue sets, alcohol burners provide a steady heat and are suitable for all types of fondue.
- Butane Burners: Offer easy adjustability and can provide a strong, steady heat, which is great for meat fondues.
- Electric Fondue Pots: These pots come with built-in heating elements and temperature controls, making it easier to maintain the correct temperature throughout the dining experience.

Ensure that whichever burner you use, it is filled with the appropriate fuel and that you are familiar with how to operate it safely.

3. Fondue Forks

Fondue forks are long, thin, and typically have two or three tines. They are designed for dipping bread, vegetables, or meat into the fondue. Each fork usually features a different colored handle, which helps guests keep track of their own fork. When selecting fondue forks, choose ones that are sturdy and have heat-resistant handles.

4. Dipping Trays and Plates

Dipping trays and small plates are essential for holding the various items to be dipped. Trays can be used to organize and separate raw meats from other dippables in meat fondue setups, while plates serve individual guests. Opt for materials that are easy to clean and can handle the slight mess fondue can create.

5. Lazy Susan

A Lazy Susan can be a useful addition for larger fondue parties. It's a rotating tray placed in the center of the table, making it easy for guests to reach different dips and dippers without having to stretch over the table or disturb other guests.

6. Sauces and Condiments Holders

For meat fondues, a variety of sauces and condiments enhance the experience. Small bowls or containers are necessary for holding these sauces, allowing guests to personalize their meal to their taste preferences.

7. Splatter Guard

When cooking meat in hot oil, a splatter guard can be placed over the pot to protect diners from oil splatters. This is especially recommended for safety and to keep the dining area clean.

8. Additional Accessories

- **Heatproof Mat or Trivet**: Protects your table surface from the heat of the fondue pot.
- **Long Matches or Lighter**: Useful for lighting alcohol or butane burners safely.
- **Thermometer**: For oil fondues, a thermometer ensures the oil is at the proper temperature for cooking meat safely.

Having the right equipment is key to ensuring your fondue meal goes smoothly and is enjoyable for all your guests. This comprehensive set of tools will prepare you for any fondue type, from a cheesy delight to a chocolate indulgence or a savory meat feast, ensuring every aspect of your fondue experience is covered.

Classic Cheese Fondue Mastery

Alpine Summit Fondue

 4 SERVINGS   21 MINUTES   10 MINUTES

This Alpine Summit Fondue captivates the essence of the Swiss highlands with a rich blend of creamy Gruyère and earthy Emmental cheeses. Infused with traditional flavors like garlic and white wine, this aromatic and velvety cheese fondue is a summit of taste that promises to elevate your dining to new peaks of enjoyment.

Equipment: Fondue pot, Wooden spoon, Fondue forks

Ingredients:

- 200g Gruyère cheese, grated
- 200g Emmental cheese, grated
- 1 clove Garlic
- 300ml Dry white wine
- 1 tbsp Cornstarch
- 2 tbsp Kirsch (cherry brandy)
- 1 pinch Nutmeg, freshly grated
- 1 pinch Ground black pepper
- 1 pinch Paprika
- 1 French Baguette, cut into bite-size cubes

Nutritional Information: Calories: 603, Protein: 38g, Carbohydrates: 6g, Fat: 42g, Fiber: 0g, Cholesterol: 189 mg, Sodium: 621 mg, Potassium: 98 mg

Directions:

1. For added taste, rub the clove of garlic inside the fondue pot and then throw it away.
2. Pour the white wine into the pot and heat gently until hot, but not boiling.
3. In a separate bowl, toss the grated cheeses with the cornstarch until they are evenly coated. This will help to thicken the fondue and prevent clumping.
4. Add the cheese to the wine gradually, swirling continually with the wooden spoon in a figure-eight pattern until the cheese is smooth and fully melted.
5. Stir in the Kirsch, nutmeg, black pepper, and a pinch of paprika, blending well.
6. Once the fondue is smooth and bubbling gently, it is ready to be served. Transfer the fondue pot to its burner at the table and adjust the flame so that the fondue remains warm but does not overcook.
7. Serve immediately with cubed French baguette or other dippers such as steamed vegetables, boiled potatoes, or apple slices.

Parisian Nights Gruyère Fondue

 4 SERVINGS   15 MINUTES   10 MINUTES

Take a trip to the heart of France with the Parisian Nights Gruyère Fondue. This classic, creamy fondue has an exquisite nutty flavor that is characteristic of Gruyère cheese, made even more delightful with a touch of French flair. Perfect for an evening filled with romance or a sophisticated gathering with friends, this fondue is sure to enchant and impress.

Equipment: Fondue pot, Whisk, Grater

Ingredients:

- 400g Gruyère cheese, freshly grated
- 200g Emmental cheese, freshly grated
- 1 Garlic clove, halved
- 300ml Dry white wine, such as a French Chablis
- 1 tbsp Cornstarch
- 2 tbsp Kirsch (cherry brandy)
- 1/2 tsp Lemon juice
- 1 pinch Ground nutmeg
- 1 pinch Ground black pepper
- 1 pinch Salt, to taste

Nutritional Information: Calories: 539, Protein: 36g, Carbohydrates: 6g, Fat: 34g, Fiber: 0g, Cholesterol: 109 mg, Sodium: 298 mg, Potassium: 100 mg

Directions:

1. After rubbing the chopped sides of the garlic clove inside the fondue pot, throw away the garlic.
2. After rubbing the chopped sides of the garlic clove inside the fondue pot, throw away the garlic.
3. In a small bowl, mix the cornstarch with the Kirsch to form a smooth slurry.
4. Gradually add the Gruyère and Emmental cheese to the wine, stirring constantly with a whisk in a zigzag pattern (rather than a circular motion) to prevent the cheese from balling up. Keep going until all of the cheeses are mixed and melted.
5. Stir in the cornstarch-Kirsch mixture into the cheese. Stir continuously and simmer over low heat for 3 to 5 minutes, or until the fondue starts to thicken.
6. Add pepper, salt, and nutmeg to taste. Mix thoroughly.
7. Once the fondue is smooth and thickened, take the pot to the table and set it on its burner. Keep the fondue warm on a low setting.
8. Serve with assorted dippers like cubed French bread, blanched vegetables, and sliced fruits.

Tuscan Fontina Dream

 4 SERVINGS   20 MINUTES   10 MINUTES

Immerse your senses in the rolling hills of Tuscany with this Tuscan Fontina Dream fondue. It combines the smooth, nutty flavors of Fontina cheese with the earthy undertones of porcini mushrooms and a hint of Italian herbs, creating an authentically Italian fondue experience. Ideal for a cozy gathering or a romantic dinner, this recipe promises to transport you and your guests to an Italian countryside with each delectable dip.

Equipment: Fondue pot, Wooden spoon, Fondue forks or skewers for dipping

Ingredients:

- 200g Fontina cheese, shredded
- 1 clove Garlic, halved
- 150ml Dry white wine, such as Pinot Grigio
- 2 tsp Cornstarch
- 1 tbsp Water
- 1 tbsp Porcini mushrooms, finely chopped and rehydrated
- ½ tsp Italian seasoning
- Freshly ground black pepper, to taste
- Pinch of nutmeg
- French baguette, Granny Smith apples, and vegetables (such as blanched broccoli or asparagus), for dipping

Nutritional Information: Calories: 271, Protein: 14g, Carbohydrates: 6g, Fat: 19g, Fiber: 0.5g, Cholesterol: 67 mg, Sodium: 619 mg, Potassium: 92 mg

Directions:

1. After rubbing the chopped sides of the garlic clove inside the fondue pot, throw away the garlic.
2. Pour the white wine into the pot and heat over a medium flame until hot, but not boiling.
3. Gradually stir in the shredded Fontina cheese until melted and smooth, ensuring to stir constantly to prevent any cheese from sticking to the bottom of the pot.
4. In a small bowl, dissolve the cornstarch in the water to make a slurry. Stir until the fondue starts to thicken after adding this to the cheese mixture.
5. Stir in the chopped porcini mushrooms, Italian seasoning, freshly ground black pepper, and nutmeg, and continue to cook for a couple more minutes until everything is heated through and well combined.
6. Once ready, reduce the heat to low (or transfer to a candle-lit fondue stand if not cooking directly at the table) and serve with cubes of French baguette, slices of Granny Smith apples, and your selected vegetables for dipping.

Savoie's Secret Fondue

 4 SERVINGS   25 MINUTES   15 MINUTES

Discover the heart of the French Alps with Savoie's Secret Fondue, a rich and creamy concoction that encapsulates the traditional flavors of the Savoie region in France. This fondue combines classic cheeses and a hint of crisp white wine, perfect for a cozy evening or a dinner party with friends.

Equipment: Fondue pot, Heat source (burner or sterno), Fondue forks

Ingredients:

- 200g Gruyère, shredded
- 200g Beaufort, shredded
- 200g Emmental, shredded
- 1 garlic clove, halved
- 300ml dry white wine, such as Apremont or Chignin
- 1 tsp lemon juice
- 2 tsp cornstarch
- 3 tbsp kirsch (cherry brandy)
- 1/4 tsp ground nutmeg
- Freshly ground black pepper, to taste
- A pinch of salt, if needed
- 1 baguette, cut into bite-sized cubes

Nutritional Information: Calories: 698, Protein: 45g, Carbohydrates: 9g, Fat: 42g, Fiber: 0g, Cholesterol: 184 mg, Sodium: 912 mg, Potassium: 168 mg

Directions:

1. Using the cut sides of the garlic clove, rub the inside of the fondue pot. Leave the garlic in the pot for added flavor or remove it if preferred.
2. Transfer the white wine and lemon juice into the fondue pot and slowly heat over medium heat until heated through, without boiling.
3. To ensure equal coating, mix the shredded cheeses with the cornstarch in a basin.
4. Gradually add the cheese to the pot, stirring constantly in a figure-8 pattern to prevent clumping, until the cheese is completely melted and the mixture is smooth.
5. Add the kirsch, grated nutmeg, and black pepper, and simmer over low heat for an additional five minutes, or until the fondue is thick and creamy.
6. Add a small teaspoon of salt to adjust the seasoning if needed.
7. Place the fondue pot on its burner or sterno to keep warm at the table. Spear cubes of bread onto fondue forks and dip into the cheese mixture.

Hoppy Cheddar Delight

 4 SERVINGS 20 MINUTES 15 MINUTES

Dive into the robust flavors of this Hoppy Cheddar Delight fondue, a perfect harmony of sharp cheddar cheese and the aromatic nuances of your favorite hoppy beer. Whether it's ale, lager, or stout, this fondue will create a memorable experience with its vibrant taste and gooey texture, making it a perfect centerpiece for any gathering.

Equipment: Fondue pot, Wooden spoon, Measuring cups and spoons

Ingredients:

- 12 oz Sharp cheddar cheese, shredded
- 1 tbsp Cornstarch
- 1 cup Hoppy beer (ale, lager, or stout)
- 2 tsp Dijon mustard
- 1 clove Garlic, halved
- 1/4 tsp Paprika
- Pinch Cayenne pepper
- Freshly ground black pepper, to taste

Nutritional Information: Calories: 386, Protein: 23g, Carbohydrates: 4g, Fat: 31g, Fiber: 0g, Cholesterol: 94 mg, Sodium: 621 mg, Potassium: 97 mg

Directions:

1. In a bowl, toss the shredded cheddar cheese with cornstarch until evenly coated. This helps to thicken the fondue and prevent the cheese from clumping.
2. After rubbing the chopped side of the garlic clove all over the fondue pot, throw it away.
3. Pour the hoppy beer into the pot and heat over a medium flame until hot, but not boiling.
4. To keep the cheese from balling up, add it gradually, a handful at a time, and stir continuously in a zigzag pattern as opposed to a circular one. Wait until the cheese has completely melted before adding more.
5. Add the paprika, cayenne, black pepper, and Dijon mustard once the cheese has melted completely and the mixture is smooth.
6. Stirring continually, simmer for an additional five minutes or more, or until the fondue is thick and creamy. Keep it from boiling.
7. If the fondue seems too thick, add a splash more beer until the desired consistency is reached.
8. Transfer the fondue pot to a lit burner on your table, and keep the fondue warm on a low setting.
9. Serve with your choice of dippers on skewers or fondue forks.

Mediterranean Breeze Fondue

 4 SERVINGS 25 MINUTES 15 MINUTES

Immerse your palate in the flavors of the Mediterranean with this exquisite cheese fondue. A sophisticated blend of Gruyere and Feta, accentuated by crisp white wine and fragrant herbs, creates a melting pot that is both soothingly familiar and tantalizingly exotic.

Equipment: Fondue pot, Heat-resistant stirring spoon, Fondue forks

Ingredients:

- 200g Gruyere cheese, shredded
- 100g Feta cheese, crumbled
- 1 garlic clove
- 1 cup dry white wine
- 1 tbsp cornstarch
- 2 tbsp water
- 1 tbsp fresh lemon juice
- 1 tsp dried oregano
- 1/2 tsp dried basil
- 1/4 tsp ground black pepper
- 1/4 cup kalamata olives, finely chopped
- 1/4 cup sun-dried tomatoes, finely chopped
- Fresh parsley, chopped for garnish

Nutritional Information: Calories: 380, Protein: 24g, Carbohydrates: 7g, Fat: 25g, Fiber: 0.5g, Cholesterol: 90 mg, Sodium: 710 mg, Potassium: 100 mg

Directions:

1. After rubbing the garlic clove all over the fondue pot's interior, throw the garlic away.
2. White wine and lemon juice should be added to the pot and cooked thoroughly, being cautious not to boil.
3. In a small bowl, mix cornstarch with water to create a smooth slurry.
4. Gradually add the Gruyere cheese to the wine mixture, stirring constantly in a zigzag pattern to prevent the cheese from balling up. Melting the cheese should be done slowly to ensure a smooth fondue.
5. Once the Gruyere has melted and the mixture is smooth, add the Feta cheese, stirring well until you achieve a creamy consistency.
6. Stir in the slurry to thicken the fondue, continuing to stir until everything is well-blended and smooth.
7. Add oregano, basil, black pepper, olives, and sun-dried tomatoes, mixing well.
8. Allow the fondue to cook for another 2-3 minutes, then transfer to a fondue stand with a burner.
9. Garnish with freshly chopped parsley before serving.

Smoky Mountains Fondue

 6 SERVINGS   15 MINUTES   20 MINUTES

Get ready to be transported to the heart of Appalachia with the Smoky Mountains Fondue. Combining the sharp richness of cheddar and the smoky undertones of Gouda, this recipe pays homage to smoky flavors that are reminiscent of a cozy mountain lodge fireplace. Best enjoyed with friends, this fondue adds a rustic, comforting twist to your traditional cheese fondue experience.

Equipment: Fondue pot, Whisk, Grater

Ingredients:

- 1/2 pound Smoked Gouda, shredded
- 1/2 pound Sharp cheddar cheese, shredded
- A single cup of dry white wine, such Sauvignon Blanc
- 1 tablespoon Cornstarch
- 2 cloves Garlic, minced
- 1 teaspoon Mustard powder
- 1 teaspoon Worcestershire sauce
- 1/4 teaspoon Liquid smoke (optional for extra smokiness)
- A pinch of Paprika, for garnish
- A pinch of Salt, to taste
- Fresh ground Black pepper, to taste

Nutritional Information: Calories: 380, Protein: 24g, Carbohydrates: 3g, Fat: 28g, Fiber: 0g, Cholesterol: 89 mg, Sodium: 712 mg, Potassium: 76 mg

Directions:

1. Combine both Gouda and cheddar with the cornstarch in a bowl, tossing to coat.
2. Rub the fondue pot with the garlic cloves to infuse it with garlic flavor.
3. Avoid letting the wine boil as you carefully pour it into the fondue pot and warm it over medium heat.
4. To promote even melting and avoid clumping, gradually add the cheese mixture to the pot while stirring continuously in a figure-8 pattern.
5. When the cheese has fully melted, incorporate mustard powder, Worcestershire sauce, and liquid smoke, if using.
6. Stir the fondue until it becomes creamy and smooth. Adjust consistency if necessary by adding a splash more wine or a bit of cornstarch dissolved in wine.
7. A small pinch of salt and freshly ground black pepper should be added.
8. Transfer the fondue pot to its burner, and let guests dip their chosen accompaniments using fondue forks.
9. Sprinkle a pinch of paprika over the fondue before serving.

Orchard Blue Cheese Fondue

 4 SERVINGS   15 MINUTES   10 MINUTES

Invite the bold and distinctive flavor of blue cheese into a cozy gathering with this Orchard Blue Cheese Fondue. It's a sophisticated yet rustic culinary excursion that combines the sweet, crisp notes of apple cider with the acidic bite of blue cheese and the creamy richness of traditional fondue.

Equipment: Fondue pot, Stove, Whisk

Ingredients:

- 200g Gruyère cheese, grated
- 150g Blue cheese, crumbled
- 1 tbsp Cornstarch
- 200ml Apple cider
- 1 tsp Lemon juice
- 1 Garlic clove, halved
- 1 tbsp Apple brandy (optional)
- Pinch of nutmeg
- Freshly ground black pepper, to taste
- Cubed artisan bread, for dipping
- Fresh apple slices, for dipping
- Blanched vegetables (such as broccoli, carrots, and cauliflower), for dipping

Nutritional Information: Calories: 380, Protein: 22g, Carbohydrates: 15g, Fat: 25g, Fiber: 1g, Cholesterol: 75 mg, Sodium: 650 mg, Potassium: 125 mg

Directions:

1. After rubbing the chopped sides of the garlic clove inside the fondue pot, throw away the garlic.
2. Add the lemon juice and apple cider to the pot, then heat it over medium heat until it's hot but not boiling.
3. Toss the grated Gruyère cheese and crumbled blue cheese with the cornstarch in a separate bowl to coat evenly.
4. When the cheeses are completely melted and the fondue is smooth and creamy, gradually add the cheese mixture to the saucepan and whisk continuously. Make sure to stir in a figure-eight pattern to ensure even melting.
5. Stir in the apple brandy, if using, and season with a pinch of nutmeg and freshly ground black pepper.
6. Once the mixture is bubbling gently, reduce the heat to low, just enough to keep the fondue warm.
7. Serve immediately with the cubed artisan bread, fresh apple slices, and blanched vegetables for dipping.
8. To keep the fondue smooth, occasionally stir it.

Brie Bliss with Cranberry Glaze

 4 SERVINGS 20 MINUTES 10 MINUTES

Savor the rich, creamy flavors of Brie cheese fondue paired with the sweet and tangy zing of a homemade cranberry glaze. Perfect for an elegant gathering or a cozy night in, this fondue captures the sophisticated harmony of sweet and savory.

Equipment: Fondue pot, heat source (sterno, electric, or candle), fondue forks or skewers

Ingredients:

- 1 lb Brie cheese, rinds removed and cubed
- 1/2 cup dry white wine
- 1 garlic clove, halved
- 1/2 cup cranberry juice
- 2 tbsp cornstarch
- 2 tbsp water
- 1/4 cup whole cranberries (fresh or frozen)
- 1 tsp orange zest
- 1 tbsp honey
- Salt and pepper to taste

Nutritional Information: Calories: 480, Protein: 28g, Carbohydrates: 20g, Fat: 29g, Fiber: 1g, Cholesterol: 95 mg, Sodium: 700 mg, Potassium: 200 mg

Directions:

1. Garlic halves should be rubbed into the fondue pot and then thrown out.
2. Over medium heat, warm the dry white wine until hot but not boiling. Add the cubed Brie gradually while continuing to stir with a wooden spoon until the cheese melts and becomes smooth.
3. In a small bowl, combine cornstarch and water to create a slurry. Gradually add the slurry to the cheese mixture, stirring until it thickens slightly to a rich, velvety texture.
4. In a separate saucepan, warm cranberry juice over medium heat. Add the whole cranberries and simmer until they start to burst. Stir in the orange zest and honey and continue to cook until the mixture achieves a glaze consistency. Add a dash of pepper and salt for seasoning.
5. Drizzle the cranberry glaze over the prepared cheese fondue just before serving, gently swirling it with a spoon to create a marbled effect.
6. Arrange the bread cubes, apple slices, and blanched vegetables around the fondue pot. Invite guests to spear their chosen dippers with fondue forks and dip into the Brie and cranberry glaze mixture, coating each piece generously.

Roman Holiday Mozzarella Fondue

 4 SERVINGS 20 MINUTES 10 MINUTES

Capture the fresh and sun-kissed flavors of Italy with this "Roman Holiday Mozzarella Fondue" - a luscious blend of creamy mozzarella, tangy tomatoes, and aromatic basil, all melted to perfection for a truly Mediterranean fondue experience.

Equipment: Fondue pot, Stove, Wooden spoon

Ingredients:

- 2 cups Shredded mozzarella cheese
- 1 cup Canned diced tomatoes, drained
- 1/2 cup Dry white wine
- 2 tbsp All-purpose flour
- 1 tbsp Extra virgin olive oil
- 1 Garlic clove, halved
- 2 tbsp Fresh basil, chopped
- 1/4 tsp Red pepper flakes (optional)
- Salt and black pepper to taste
- For serving: Crusty Italian bread cubes, blanched vegetables, cooked meatballs or grilled chicken pieces

Nutritional Information: Calories: 340, Protein: 21g, Carbohydrates: 8g, Fat: 24g, Fiber: 1g, Cholesterol: 45 mg, Sodium: 500 mg, Potassium: 150 mg

Directions:

1. Once the garlic clove has been halved and rubbed throughout the fondue pot, discard the garlic.
2. Heat up the olive oil in the fondue pot over medium flame. Add in the drained diced tomatoes and cook for about 5 minutes until they soften and start to break down.
3. In a separate bowl, toss the shredded mozzarella with all-purpose flour to coat. This helps in preventing the cheese from clumping.
4. Pour the dry white wine into the tomato mixture and heat until just simmering.
5. Gradually add the cheese to the pot, a handful at a time, stirring constantly in a figure-eight pattern until the cheese is completely melted and the fondue is smooth.
6. Add the red pepper flakes (if using) and chopped basil, then taste and adjust the seasoning with salt and black pepper.
7. Once the cheese has fully melted and the fondue is smooth, set the pot over a burner at the dining table to keep the fondue warm while serving.
8. Serve with cubes of crusty Italian bread, blanched vegetables, cooked meatballs, or grilled chicken pieces for dipping.

Garlic Whisper Fondue

 4 SERVINGS   15 MINUTES   10 MINUTES

Indulge in the subtle hint of garlic that gracefully complements this creamy delight. The Garlic Whisper Fondue is a romantic twist to the classic cheese fondue, perfect for those who want to relish the flavors of traditional Swiss fondue with a gentle kiss of garlic. It's an ideal match for bread, vegetables, or even a selection of meats.

Equipment: Fondue pot, Heat source (stove or fondue burner), Fondue forks or skewers, Garlic press

Ingredients:

- 200 g Gruyère cheese, shredded
- 200 g Emmental cheese, shredded
- 1 clove of garlic, minced
- 1 cup dry white wine
- 1 tsp lemon juice
- 2 tsp cornstarch
- 3 tbsp water
- 1 pinch of nutmeg
- 1 pinch of paprika
- Freshly ground black pepper to taste
- Bread cubes, for dipping

Directions:

1. To start, massage the minced garlic clove all over the fondue pot to give it a garlicky scent.
2. Transfer the lemon juice and white wine into the pot, then adjust the heat to medium. Bring it to a boil without boiling it.
3. Gradually stir in the Gruyère and Emmental cheese, continuously stirring until the cheese has completely melted and the mixture is smooth.
4. In a small bowl, dissolve the cornstarch in the water and add it to the cheese mixture to thicken, constantly stirring.
5. Once the fondue has thickened to your liking, season it with a pinch of nutmeg, paprika, and freshly ground black pepper.
6. Lower the heat source or set the fondue burner to low to keep the fondue warm while serving.
7. Serve with bread cubes and your choice of other dippables on the side.

Nutritional Information: Calories: 428, Protein: 28g, Carbohydrates: 4g, Fat: 29g, Fiber: 0g, Cholesterol: 89 mg, Sodium: 536 mg, Potassium: 108 mg

Fiery Pepper Jack Melt

 4 SERVINGS   15 MINUTES   10 MINUTES

Savor the bold flavors of this Fiery Pepper Jack Melt that blends the tangy and creamy textures of Pepper Jack cheese with a touch of heat from jalapeños and a kick of garlic, perfect for those who love their cheese fondue with a spicy twist.

Equipment: Fondue pot, Wooden spoon, Cheese grater

Ingredients:

- 1 lb Pepper Jack cheese, shredded
- 1 clove garlic, halved
- 1 cup dry white wine
- 2 tbsp cornstarch
- 2 tbsp water
- 1 tbsp pickled jalapeños, finely chopped
- 1 tsp hot sauce (optional, for extra heat)
- A pinch of black pepper
- A pinch of nutmeg
- Assorted dippers (such as cubed French bread, blanched vegetables, apples slices, and cooked sausage)

Directions:

1. Garlic halves should be rubbed into the fondue pot before being discarded.
2. Pour the white wine into the pot and heat it on medium until it's hot, but not boiling.
3. In a separate bowl, toss the shredded Pepper Jack cheese with the cornstarch to coat.
4. Gradually add the coated cheese to the wine in the fondue pot, stirring constantly in a figure-eight motion until the cheese is fully melted and smooth.
5. Stir the cornstarch and water into a slurry in a small basin and pour it into the fondue.
6. Add the chopped jalapeños, hot sauce (if using), black pepper, and nutmeg into the fondue, stirring well.
7. Once the fondue is smooth and bubbling gently, transfer the fondue pot to its burner at the table and serve with your chosen dippers.

Nutritional Information: Calories: 405, Protein: 24g, Carbohydrates: 4g, Fat: 31g, Fiber: 0g, Cholesterol: 85 mg, Sodium: 620 mg, Potassium: 70 mg

Brewmaster's Pretzel Fondue

 4 SERVINGS 15 MINUTES 20 MINUTES

This robust and malty cheese fondue draws inspiration from the hearty flavors found in a brewpub. Combining the smooth, nutty undertones of Swiss and Gruyère cheeses with the boldness of your favorite lager, this comforting fondue dips beautifully with an array of pretzel bites and crudités. It's an ooey-gooey homage to the classic bar snack, captivating beer lovers and fondue enthusiasts alike.

Equipment: Fondue pot, Whisk, Stove or portable burner

Ingredients:

- 8 oz Swiss cheese, shredded
- 8 oz Gruyère cheese, shredded
- 2 tbsp cornstarch
- 1 cup lager beer (choose a beer with a rich, deep flavor)
- 2 tbsp apple cider vinegar
- 1 tbsp Dijon mustard
- 1 clove garlic, halved
- 1 tsp Worcestershire sauce
- Freshly ground black pepper, to taste
- Pretzel bites, for dipping
- Vegetables like broccoli, cauliflowers and carrots, for dipping

Nutritional Information: Calories: 420, Protein: 28g, Carbohydrates: 10g, Fat: 28g, Fiber: 0g, Cholesterol: 100 mg, Sodium: 640 mg, Potassium: 100 mg

Directions:

1. Mix the cornstarch and Gruyère and Swiss cheeses in a medium-sized bowl until well coated. This helps thicken the fondue and prevent separation.
2. Rub the inside of the fondue pot with the cut sides of the garlic clove, then discard the garlic.
3. Transfer the lager beer into the fondue pot and warm it over a medium heat source without letting it boil.
4. Stir together the Dijon mustard and apple cider vinegar after adding them to the pot.
5. A handful at a time, gradually add the cheese mixture, stirring continuously after each addition until the cheese has melted completely and the fondue is smooth.
6. Add the black pepper and Worcestershire sauce and stir. Stir the mixture continuously until it becomes creamy and begins to bubble gently.
7. Reduce the flame to low to keep the fondue warm for dipping.
8. Serve immediately with pretzel bites and your selection of vegetables.

Swiss Bliss Emmental Fondue

 4 SERVINGS 20 MINUTES 10 MINUTES

Dive into the heart of Swiss cuisine with this classic cheese fondue, embraced by the smooth, nutty flavors of Emmental. Gather friends and family around the pot for a cozy night in, dipping crusty bread into this rich, melted delight for a true taste of Swiss Bliss.

Equipment: Fondue pot, Fondue forks, Stove or burner

Ingredients:

- 200g Emmental cheese, grated
- 200g Gruyère cheese, grated
- 1 clove garlic, halved
- 300ml dry white wine (such as Sauvignon Blanc)
- 1 tbsp lemon juice
- 2 tsp cornstarch
- 1 tbsp kirsch (cherry brandy)
- 1 pinch ground nutmeg
- 1 pinch paprika
- 1 pinch freshly ground black pepper
- 1 loaf crusty bread, cut into bite-sized cubes for dipping

Nutritional Information: Calories: 499, Protein: 30g, Carbohydrates: 9g, Fat: 29g, Fiber: 0g, Cholesterol: 156 mg, Sodium: 619 mg, Potassium: 126 mg

Directions:

1. Rub the inside of the fondue pot with the halves of garlic for fragrant seasoning.
2. After adding the lemon juice and white wine to the pot, cook it over medium heat without letting it boil.
3. Reduce the heat to low and gradually add the grated Emmental and Gruyère cheeses to the pot, stirring continuously in a figure-eight pattern to ensure even melting and prevent clumping.
4. Dissolve the cornstarch in the kirsch and then stir into the cheese mixture.
5. Continue to cook on a low heat while stirring until the fondue mixture becomes smooth and creamy.
6. Season with nutmeg, paprika, and black pepper to taste.
7. Once the fondue is ready, transfer the pot to a burner at the table and adjust the flame to keep the fondue warm but not too hot.
8. Serve with the pieces of crusty bread for dipping. Use fondue forks to spear the bread, then dip and swirl in the cheese fondue.

Bordeaux Bliss Fondue

 4 SERVINGS 20 MINUTES 15 MINUTES

Delve into the rich textures and exquisite taste of the Bordeaux Bliss Fondue, a classic cheese fondue with an elegant twist inspired by the famous French wine region. Infused with bold red wine and a blend of fine cheeses, this sumptuous dish is guaranteed to captivate your palate and transport you to the heart of Bordeaux with each bite.

Equipment: Fondue Pot, Wooden Spoon, Garlic Press (optional)

Ingredients:

- 200g Gruyère cheese, shredded
- 200g Emmental cheese, shredded
- 1 tbsp Cornstarch
- 1 cup Bordeaux wine
- 1 clove Garlic, halved
- 1 tsp Lemon juice
- 1 pinch Nutmeg, freshly grated
- 1 pinch White pepper

Nutritional Information: Calories: 420, Protein: 28g, Carbohydrates: 5g, Fat: 22g, Fiber: 0g, Cholesterol: 95 mg, Sodium: 390 mg, Potassium: 125 mg

Directions:

1. Mix Gruyère and Emmental cheese with cornstarch in a small bowl to coat evenly for a smoother fondue.
2. Rub the inside of the fondue pot with garlic halves to infuse flavor, then discard the garlic.
3. Heat Bordeaux wine in the pot on medium until hot but not boiling to preserve the alcohol for flavor.
4. Add lemon juice to the wine to help stabilize the fondue and ensure a silky texture.
5. Gradually add the cheese to the wine, stirring in a figure-eight pattern to melt evenly and prevent clumps.
6. Once the cheese is melted and smooth, season with nutmeg and white pepper, stirring well.
7. Adjust the thickness by adding more wine if necessary.
8. Keep the fondue warm on low heat, use fondue forks to dip and swirl your chosen items in the cheese.

Neuchâtel Nectar Fondue

 4 SERVINGS 15 MINUTES 10 MINUTES

Indulge in the creamy dreaminess of Neuchâtel Nectar Fondue, an homage to the Swiss canton renowned for its rich dairy heritage. This classic fondue recipe blends earthy Gruyère with creamy Emmental, sharp Neuchâtel cheese, and a hint of garlic, all melted into a smooth, velvety dip that exemplifies comfort food at its finest.

Equipment: Fondue pot, Heat source (burner or candle), Fondue forks

Ingredients:

- 8 oz Gruyère cheese, grated
- 8 oz Emmental cheese, grated
- 4 oz Neuchâtel cheese, finely diced
- 1 cup dry white wine, such as a Swiss Fendant
- 2 tsp cornstarch
- 1 garlic clove, halved
- 1 tbsp lemon juice
- 1 pinch freshly ground nutmeg
- 1 pinch white pepper
- 2 tsp kirsch (cherry brandy), optional
- (

Nutritional Information: Calories: 520, Protein: 35g, Carbohydrates: 5g, Fat: 38g, Fiber: 0g, Cholesterol: 105 mg, Sodium: 620 mg, Potassium: 200 mg

Directions:

1. Rub the inside of the fondue pot with the cut sides of the garlic clove to impart its flavor. Discard the garlic or leave it at the bottom of the pot for a stronger taste.
2. Heat the dry white wine with lemon juice in the fondue pot over medium heat until hot but not boiling.
3. In a bowl, toss together the grated Gruyère, Emmental, and cornstarch until the cheese is evenly coated. This helps to stabilize and thicken the fondue.
4. To keep the cheese from clumping and to promote even melting, gradually add the cheese mixture to the pot while stirring continuously in a figure-eight pattern.
5. Once the cheese begins to melt, add the Neuchâtel cheese, continuing to stir gently until completely smooth and creamy.
6. Season with nutmeg and white pepper, adjusting to taste. Stir in the kirsch, if using, for a smooth finish and added depth of flavor.
7. Reduce the heat to its lowest setting to keep the fondue warm and liquid without overheating.
8. Serve immediately, placing the fondue pot over a burner or candle at the table. Provide guests with fondue forks to dip their chosen accompaniments into the Neuchâtel Nectar Fondue.

Rustic Raclette Fondue

 4 SERVINGS   20 MINUTES   10 MINUTES

Savor the warm, gooey goodness of Rustic Raclette Fondue, an homage to the Swiss tradition enjoyed in the comfort of your home. This rich, velvety fondue pairs perfectly with a variety of dippers, from crusty bread to fresh vegetables, offering an indulgent experience that's ideal for gatherings or a cozy night in.

Equipment: Fondue pot, Wooden spoon, Chafing dish (for serving)

Ingredients:

- 1 clove Garlic, halved
- 1 cup Dry white wine
- 1 tbsp Lemon juice
- 1 lb Raclette cheese, grated
- 2 tbsp Cornstarch
- 2 tbsp Kirsch (cherry brandy)
- Pinch of Nutmeg
- Freshly ground black Pepper, to taste

Nutritional Information: Calories: 450, Protein: 28g, Carbohydrates: 4g, Fat: 34g, Fiber: 0g, Cholesterol: 89 mg, Sodium: 620 mg, Potassium: Additional info not available

Directions:

1. Rub the inside of the fondue pot with the halves of garlic to infuse it with flavor.
2. Over medium heat, pour the white wine and lemon juice into the fondue pot and warm gently until hot, but not boiling.
3. In a separate bowl, toss the grated raclette cheese with cornstarch to evenly coat.
4. To avoid the cheese from balling up, gradually add the cheese to the saucepan while stirring continuously in a zigzag pattern rather than a circular one.
5. Continue stirring until the cheese is fully melted and the mixture is smooth and slightly bubbling.
6. Stir in the Kirsch, a pinch of nutmeg, and add black pepper to taste, blending well.
7. Reduce heat to low (or transfer to a chafing dish if not using an electric fondue pot) and serve immediately. Keep the fondue warm on a low flame to maintain its smooth texture as you dip.
8. To enjoy, spear dippers onto fondue forks and swirl in the cheese mixture.

Après-Ski Gorgonzola Fondue

 4 SERVINGS   15 MINUTES   10 MINUTES

This Après-Ski Gorgonzola Fondue is the perfect way to warm up and relax after a day on the slopes. The creamy Gorgonzola blends exquisitely with white wine and garlic, creating a rich and indulgent cheese fondue that's both comforting and sophisticated.

Equipment: Fondue pot, Heat source (like a burner or candle), Fondue forks or skewers, Mixing bowl

Ingredients:

- 200g Gorgonzola cheese, crumbled
- 200g Swiss Emmental cheese, shredded
- 200g Swiss Gruyère cheese, shredded
- 300ml dry white wine
- 1 tbsp cornstarch
- 1 garlic clove, halved
- 2 tbsp Kirsch (cherry brandy)
- 1/4 tsp ground nutmeg
- Freshly ground black pepper, to taste

Nutritional Information: Calories: 560, Protein: 34g, Carbohydrates: 8g, Fat: 41g, Fiber: 0g, Cholesterol: 94 mg, Sodium: 712 mg, Potassium: 150 mg

Directions:

1. After giving the fondue pot a flavor boost by rubbing the garlic halves inside, throw the garlic away.
2. Transfer the wine into the fondue pot and warm it up gradually without letting it boil.
3. In a mixing bowl, toss together the Gruyère, Emmental, and Gorgonzola cheeses with the cornstarch to coat evenly.
4. Gradually add the cheese mixture to the hot wine, stirring constantly in a zigzag pattern (not a circular motion) to prevent the cheese from balling up, until the cheeses are melted and the fondue is smooth and bubbling.
5. Stir in the Kirsch, nutmeg, and black pepper. Stir the ingredients continuously until it becomes smooth and creamy. Do not let it boil.
6. Once the fondue is ready, reduce the heat to low (if using a burner) or maintain a gentle heat (if using a candle) to keep the fondue warm.
7. Serve the fondue immediately with an assortment of dipping items such as chunks of crusty bread, apple wedges, and boiled baby potatoes.

Belgian Beer and Bacon Fondue

 4 SERVINGS 20 MINUTES 15 MINUTES

Embrace the heartiness of Belgian flavors with this indulgent Belgian Beer and Bacon Fondue. Melted cheese couples with the rich depth of a good Belgian ale, punctuated by the smoky saltiness of bacon for a memorable dip that's perfect for a cozy evening or entertaining friends.

Equipment: Fondue pot, Stove, Mixing bowl

Ingredients:

- 1 cup Belgian ale (preferably a blond or amber variety)
- 8 oz Gruyère cheese, shredded
- 8 oz Emmental cheese, shredded
- 8 oz smoked bacon, cooked and chopped
- 2 tbsp cornstarch
- 1 clove garlic, halved
- 1 tsp mustard powder
- 1 tbsp lemon juice
- Dash of nutmeg
- Freshly ground black pepper, to taste

Nutritional Information: Calories: 587, Protein: 34g, Carbohydrates: 8g, Fat: 43g, Fiber: 0g, Cholesterol: 99 mg, Sodium: 814 mg, Potassium: 127 mg

Directions:

1. To give the fondue a hint of garlic flavor, rub the interior of the pot with the cut garlic clove.
2. Pour the Belgian ale into the pot and heat gently on the stove until warm but not boiling.
3. In the mixing bowl, toss the shredded Gruyère and Emmental cheese with the cornstarch until evenly coated. This helps to thicken the fondue and prevent separation.
4. Gradually add the cheese mixture to the warm beer, stirring constantly in a figure-eight pattern for even melting and to stop it from sticking to the bottom.
5. Add the lemon juice, nutmeg, and mustard powder as the cheese starts to melt. Stirring continuously will smooth out the mixture.
6. As the fondue becomes creamy and smooth, mix in the chopped smoked bacon, saving a little to sprinkle on top for presentation.
7. Add freshly ground black pepper to taste when seasoning.
8. When fully incorporated and creamy, transfer the fondue pot to its burner at the table to keep warm. Adjust the burner to ensure the fondue stays warm but does not overcook.
9. Serve with an assortment of dippers such as chunks of crusty bread, blanched vegetables, or slices of apple for a delightful contrast of flavors.

Harvest Apple Cheddar Fondue

  20 MINUTES 10 MINUTES

This Harvest Apple Cheddar Fondue combines the sharp and rich flavors of aged cheddar with the sweet crispness of autumn apples, creating a warm, comforting, and delectable dip that is perfect for a cozy evening. Enjoy the harmonious balance of savory cheese and sweet apple cider that envelop every bite of your dipped bread or vegetable.

Equipment: Fondue pot, Wooden spoon, Cheese grater, Cutting board, Knife

Ingredients:

- 1 lb Sharp cheddar cheese, shredded
- 2 tbsp Cornstarch
- 1 cup Apple cider
- ½ tsp Dijon mustard
- ¼ tsp Ground nutmeg
- 1 pinch Cayenne pepper (optional)
- 2 tbsp Apple brandy (optional)
- Cubed French bread, granny smith apples, and vegetables, for dipping

Nutritional Information: Calories: 400, Protein: 24g, Carbohydrates: 10g, Fat: 29g, Fiber: 0g, Cholesterol: 100 mg, Sodium: 720 mg, Potassium: 98 mg

Directions:

1. Toss the shredded cheddar cheese and cornstarch in a medium-sized basin until well coated. This helps thicken the fondue and ensures a smooth texture.
2. Heat the apple cider in the fondue pot over medium heat until it starts to simmer. Do not boil to avoid evaporating too much liquid.
3. In order to promote equal melting and avoid clumping, turn down the heat to low and gradually add the cheese to the simmering cider, stirring continuously in a figure-eight pattern.
4. Stir in the Dijon mustard, nutmeg, and cayenne pepper (if using). Once the cheese has melted completely and the fondue sauce is smooth, keep cooking and stirring.
5. If the fondue is too thick, add additional apple cider, one tablespoon at a time, until the desired consistency is reached.
6. For an extra depth of flavor, stir in the apple brandy (if using) just before serving.
7. Serve the fondue warm with cubes of French bread, slices of granny smith apple, and an assortment of vegetables like broccoli, cauliflower, and carrots.

Herbes de Provence Fondue

 4 SERVINGS   15 MINUTES   10 MINUTES

A delightful twist on traditional cheese fondue, the Herbes de Provence Fondue introduces the aromatic flavors of the French countryside to warm, melted cheese. Perfect for a cozy night in or a gathering with friends, this fondue offers a herbaceous flavor profile that pairs wonderfully with an array of dippables.

Equipment: Fondue pot, Whisk, Grater, Garlic press (optional)

Ingredients:

- 200g Gruyère cheese, grated
- 200g Emmentaler cheese, grated
- 200g Comté cheese, grated
- 1 garlic clove, halved
- 300ml dry white wine
- 20ml kirsch (cherry brandy)
- 2 tsp cornstarch
- 2 tbsp water
- 1/2 tsp lemon juice
- 1/2 tsp Herbes de Provence
- Pinch of nutmeg
- Freshly ground pepper, to taste
- 1 loaf crusty bread, cut into bite-size cubes (for serving)

Nutritional Information: Calories: 550, Protein: 36g, Carbohydrates: 18g, Fat: 34g, Fiber: 1g, Cholesterol: 100 mg, Sodium: 620 mg, Potassium: 200 mg

Directions:

1. After rubbing the halved clove of garlic all over the fondue pot, throw the garlic away.
2. Pour the dry white wine and lemon juice into the pot and heat until hot, but not boiling.
3. In a bowl, combine the cornstarch with water to create a slurry.
4. Gradually add the grated cheeses to the wine mixture, stirring constantly in a zigzag pattern (not a circular motion) to prevent the cheese from balling up. Once the cheeses are all melted and blended, stir.
5. Stir in the cornstarch slurry, Herbes de Provence, nutmeg, and freshly ground pepper, and continue to cook until the mixture becomes smooth and creamy. Do not let it boil.
6. Once the cheese is smooth, add the kirsch and stir well.
7. Transfer the pot to a fondue burner set on a table where everyone can reach.
8. Serve immediately with cubes of crusty bread for dipping. Use long fondue forks to dip and swirl the bread cubes in the cheese.

Saffron Elegance Fondue

 4 SERVINGS   20 MINUTES   10 MINUTES

Indulge in the opulence of "Saffron Elegance Fondue," a refined twist on the classic cheese fondue that incorporates the luxurious taste of saffron. This sumptuous blend of rich cheeses is infused with the exotic aroma and golden color of saffron, delivering a gourmet dining experience that is as visually appealing as it is delicious. Perfect for a special occasion or a sophisticated dinner party, this fondue will enchant your taste buds and leave a lasting impression.

Equipment: Fondue pot, Small bowl, Whisk

Ingredients:

- 1 pinch Saffron threads
- 1 tbsp Hot water
- 200g Gruyère cheese, grated
- 200g Emmental cheese, grated
- 200g Vacherin Fribourgeois cheese, grated
- 1 Garlic clove, halved
- 300ml Dry white wine
- 1 tsp Lemon juice
- 2 tsp Cornstarch
- 2 tbsp Kirsch (cherry brandy)
- Ground pepper to taste
- Grated nutmeg to taste

Nutritional Information: Calories: 560, Protein: 36g, Carbohydrates: 4g, Fat: 41g, Fiber: 0g, Cholesterol: 105 mg, Sodium: 620 mg, Potassium: 100 mg

Directions:

1. Place the saffron threads in a small bowl with the hot water and allow them to steep for 10 minutes to release their color and aroma.
2. Rub the inside of the fondue pot with the cut sides of the garlic clove, then discard the garlic.
3. Heat the saucepan until it is hot but not boiling, then add the white wine and lemon juice.
4. Lower the heat and gradually add the grated cheeses, stirring constantly in a zigzag pattern to prevent cheese from balling up, until the cheeses are melted and the mixture is smooth.
5. In a small bowl, dissolve the cornstarch in the Kirsch to create a slurry.
6. Stir the saffron, including its soaking water, into the cheese mixture.
7. Add the cornstarch slurry to the fondue pot, and continue to cook and stir for 2-4 minutes or until the fondue begins to thicken.
8. Season with ground pepper and grated nutmeg to taste.
9. Serve immediately, ensuring the fondue remains warm to maintain its smooth texture.

Truffled Fontina Velvet

 4 SERVINGS   15 MINUTES   10 MINUTES

Indulge in the rich, silky elegance of Truffled Fontina Velvet, a fondue that pairs the smooth, nutty flavor of Fontina cheese with the earthy sophistication of black truffles. This luxurious dish is a perfect centerpiece for an intimate gathering, promising to tantalize the palate with its decadent blend of tastes and textures.

Equipment: Fondue pot, Wooden spoon, Grater

Ingredients:

- 1 garlic clove, halved
- 1 and 1/2 cups dry white wine
- 1 tbsp lemon juice
- 12 oz Fontina cheese, grated
- 2 oz Gruyère cheese, grated
- 2 tsp cornstarch
- 2 tbsp truffle oil
- 1 tsp freshly ground black pepper
- A pinch of nutmeg
- Fresh black truffles for garnish (optional)

Nutritional Information: Calories: Approximately 450, Protein: 28g, Carbohydrates: 6g, Fat: 32g, Fiber: 0g, Cholesterol: 100 mg, Sodium: 620 mg, Potassium: 120 mg

Directions:

1. Cut sides of the garlic clove should be rubbed within the fondue pot; discard the garlic after use.
2. Over medium heat, add the white wine and lemon juice to the fondue pot, warming until hot, but not boiling.
3. In a bowl, combine the grated Fontina and Gruyère cheeses with the cornstarch, tossing to coat evenly.
4. A handful at a time, gradually add the cheese mixture to the pot and stir continuously until the cheeses melt and the mixture is smooth and velvety.
5. Stir in the truffle oil, ground black pepper, and nutmeg, mixing well to ensure an even flavor throughout the fondue.
6. Once the fondue is smooth and fully blended, it's ready to serve.
7. Garnish with thin shavings of fresh black truffles if available for an extra touch of luxury.

Champagne and Sharp Cheddar Fondue

 4 SERVINGS   20 MINUTES   10 MINUTES

This fondue is the perfect blend of elegant and comforting. The sharpness of the cheddar pairs wonderfully with the light, effervescent quality of champagne, creating a sophisticated yet cozy dish that will dazzle on any occasion.

Equipment: Fondue pot, Whisk, Stove

Ingredients:

- 1 cup Champagne
- 1 garlic clove, halved
- 1 lb Sharp cheddar cheese, shredded
- 2 tbsp Cornstarch
- 1 tbsp Lemon juice
- 1/4 tsp Ground nutmeg
- 1/4 tsp Ground black pepper
- Sourdough bread and various vegetables, for dipping

Nutritional Information: Calories: 400, Protein: 25g, Carbohydrates: 10g, Fat: 24g, Fiber: 0g, Cholesterol: 60 mg, Sodium: 720 mg, Potassium: 100 mg

Directions:

1. Rub the garlic halves around the inside of the fondue pot, then discard.
2. Over medium heat, pour the champagne into the pot and warm it gently, but do not allow it to boil.
3. Toss the shredded cheddar cheese with the cornstarch until the pieces are evenly coated.
4. Gradually add the cheese to the pot, stirring constantly with a whisk. Continue to stir until the cheese is completely melted and the mixture is smooth.
5. Stir in the lemon juice, ground nutmeg, and black pepper, continuing to stir until everything is thoroughly combined and the fondue is creamy and smooth.
6. Turn down the heat to low and serve right away with sourdough bread chunks and a variety of veggies for dipping. Keep the fondue warm to maintain a smooth texture.

Four-Cheese Harmony Fondue

 4-6 SERVINGS 15 MINUTES 10 MINUTES

Indulge in a symphony of flavors with the Four-Cheese Harmony Fondue, where the boldness of aged cheddar meets the creaminess of Gruyère, the tang of Emmentaler, and the distinctive tinge of Roquefort. Perfect for cheese connoisseurs and fondue enthusiasts alike, this rich and decadent treat is sure to be the centerpiece of any gathering.

Equipment: Fondue pot, Wooden stirring spoon, Fondue forks

Ingredients:

- 200g Aged Cheddar, shredded
- 200g Gruyère, shredded
- 150g Emmentaler, shredded
- 100g Roquefort, crumbled
- 2 tbsp Cornstarch
- 1 clove Garlic, halved
- 1 cup Dry white wine
- 2 tbsp Lemon juice
- 1 tbsp Brandy (optional)
- 1/4 tsp Nutmeg
- Freshly ground black pepper, to taste
- 1 pinch Paprika
- 1 loaf French bread, cut into bite-sized cubes for dipping
- Assorted vegetables (bell peppers, broccoli, carrots), optional for dipping

Directions:

1. To add flavor, rub the halved clove of garlic all over the inside of the fondue pot.
2. Pour the lemon juice and white wine into the fondue pot and heat over medium heat, being careful not to boil.
3. Combine the cheddar, Gruyère, Emmentaler, and Roquefort with the cornstarch in a separate bowl, ensuring all the cheese is lightly coated.
4. To keep the cheese from balling up, gradually add the cheese mixture to the pot while stirring continuously in a zigzag pattern as opposed to a circular one.
5. Once the cheeses have melted and the fondue is smooth, stir in the brandy (if using), nutmeg, a touch of black pepper, and paprika.
6. When the fondue is bubbling gently, it's ready to serve. Adjust the fondue burner to keep the cheese warm but not boiling.
7. Spear French bread cubes or vegetables using fondue forks and dip them into the cheese mixture.

Nutritional Information: Calories: 400, Protein: 25g, Carbohydrates: 3g, Fat: 31g, Fiber: 0g, Cholesterol: 90 mg,

Spiced Wine and Swiss Fondue

 4 SERVINGS 20 MINUTES 15 MINUTES

This Spiced Wine and Swiss Fondue melds the robust flavors of a smooth red wine infused with spices paired with the rich tapestry of Swiss cheese. The slight undertones of cinnamon and clove dance harmoniously with the cheese's creaminess, culminating in a comforting and aromatic twist on the classic fondue recipe. Perfect for an evening of sophistication and warmth, this fondue will surely impress your guests with its depth of flavor and elegance.

Equipment: Fondue pot, Wooden spoon, Stove (or fondue burner)

Ingredients:

- 200g Gruyère cheese, grated
- 200g Emmentaler cheese, grated
- 200ml Dry red wine (like a Merlot or Pinot Noir)
- 1 Garlic clove, halved
- 1 Tbsp Cornstarch
- 1 Tbsp Water
- 2 Tbsp Kirsch (cherry brandy, optional)
- 1/4 tsp Grated nutmeg
- 1/4 tsp Paprika
- 1/4 tsp Freshly ground black pepper
- 1 pinch Cinnamon
- 1 pinch Ground cloves
- Bread cubes, for dipping

Directions:

1. Rub the halved garlic clove all over the inside of the fondue pot to season it, then discard the garlic.
2. Pour the red wine into the fondue pot and heat it gently on the stove until it is hot, but not boiling.
3. In a bowl, mix the cornstarch with water to make a slurry, and set aside.
4. Gradually add the Gruyère and Emmentaler cheese to the pot, stirring constantly in a zigzag pattern (not a round motion) to prevent the cheese from balling up. Wait until the cheese has mostly melted before adding more.
5. Once all the cheese is melted and smooth, stir in the cornstarch slurry to help thicken the fondue. If using, add the Kirsch at this stage.
6. Season the fondue with the nutmeg, paprika, black pepper, cinnamon, and cloves, adjusting to taste. Stir well until all the spices are evenly distributed.
7. When the mixture is smooth and bubbling gently, transfer the fondue pot to a fondue burner set on low or a candle, if serving immediately.
8. Serve the spiced wine and Swiss fondue with cubes of bread for dipping.

Nutritional Information: Calories: 478, Protein: 30g, Carbohydrates: 3g, Fat: 36g, Fiber: 0g, Cholesterol: 94 mg, Sodium: 621 mg, Potassium: 108 mg

Bourbon and Smoked Gouda Fondue

 4 SERVINGS   10 MINUTES   15 MINUTES

Experience the decadent pairing of rich bourbon and smoky gouda cheese in this sophisticated fondue. Perfect for entertaining, this twist on a classic will surely impress with its bold flavors and creamy texture.

Equipment: Fondue pot, Wooden spoon, Whisk

Ingredients:

- 1 cup Dry white wine
- 8 oz Smoked gouda cheese, shredded
- 4 oz Sharp cheddar cheese, shredded
- 2 tbsp Cornstarch
- 1/4 cup Bourbon
- 1/4 tsp Paprika
- 1/4 tsp Garlic powder
- 1/4 tsp Mustard powder
- Salt and black pepper to taste
- For Dipping: Cubed French bread, blanched broccoli, apple slices, or any other dip-ables of your choice.

Nutritional Information: Calories: 360, Protein: 18g, Carbohydrates: 5g, Fat: 20g, Fiber: 0g, Cholesterol: 90 mg, Sodium: 540 mg, Potassium: 80 mg

Directions:

1. Pour the dry white wine into the fondue pot and heat it gently over medium heat, taking care not to boil it.
2. Fill the fondue pot with the dry white wine and warm it over medium heat, without letting it boil.
3. Add the bourbon to the fondue pot and allow it to heat with the wine for a minute, ensuring it doesn't boil.
4. A gentle medium heat should be used to gently warm the dry white wine in the fondue pot, being careful not to let it boil. Wait until each batch of cheese is melted before adding more.
5. Stir in the paprika, mustard powder, and garlic powder once the cheese has melted completely and the mixture is smooth. To taste, add salt and black pepper for seasoning.
6. Continue to cook on low heat for about 5–10 minutes, stirring frequently, until the fondue is smooth and creamy.
7. To keep the fondue warm while serving, turn down the heat to the lowest level. Serve with a platter of dip-ables like chunks of French bread, blanched broccoli, and apple slices.

Ciderhouse Fondue

 4 SERVINGS   20 MINUTES   15 MINUTES

Warm up your evening with a uniquely tangy twist on a traditional cheese fondue. Our Ciderhouse Fondue brings together the rich, comforting flavors of melted cheese with the crisp, fruity notes of apple cider, perfect for dipping a variety of breads, fruits, or vegetables.

Equipment: Fondue pot, Whisk, Garlic press (optional)

Ingredients:

- 1 cup Dry hard cider
- 1 lb. Gruyère cheese, grated
- 1/2 lb. Sharp cheddar cheese, grated
- 1 tbsp Cornstarch
- 1 Garlic clove, peeled
- 1 tsp Dijon mustard
- Dash Nutmeg, grate fresh to taste
- Sea salt and fresh ground pepper, to taste
- To serve: Cubed French bread, sliced apples, blanched broccoli, or other dipping items of your choice

Nutritional Information: Calories: 520, Protein: 31g, Carbohydrates: 6g, Fat: 38g, Fiber: 0g, Cholesterol: 105 mg, Sodium: 620 mg, Potassium: 120 mg

Directions:

1. Apply some garlic powder into the fondue pot to give it some taste. You can use a garlic press and add the garlic directly to the pot for a stronger taste.
2. To add flavor to the fondue pot, add a little garlic powder.
3. In a bowl, toss the grated Gruyère and cheddar cheese with the cornstarch until evenly coated. This helps to thicken the fondue and prevent the cheese from clumping.
4. Gradually add the cheese to the hot cider in the fondue pot, stirring constantly with a whisk. Stir until the fondue sauce is smooth and the cheese has melted completely.
5. Once the cheese has melted fully and the fondue sauce is smooth, stir.
6. Once the fondue is ready, keep it warm over a low flame. Serve with your choice of dippable items such as cubed French bread, sliced apples, and blanched broccoli.

Greek Isle Feta Fondue

 4 SERVINGS   20 MINUTES   10 MINUTES

The Greek Isle Feta Fondue will transport your taste buds to the Mediterranean. This twist on classic cheese fondue incorporates the tangy and crumbly goodness of feta cheese accented with the flavors of dill, lemon, and a hint of ouzo for an unforgettable dining experience.

Equipment: Fondue pot, Wooden spoon, Cheese grater, Mixing bowl

Ingredients:

- 8 oz Feta cheese, crumbled
- 1 cup Gruyère cheese, shredded
- 2 tbsp Cornstarch
- 1 clove Garlic, halved
- 1 cup Dry white wine
- 1 tsp Lemon zest
- 1 tbsp Fresh dill, chopped
- 1 tbsp Ouzo or other anise-flavored liqueur (optional)
- Freshly ground black pepper, to taste
- Crusty bread, vegetables, and grilled meats for dipping

Nutritional Information: Calories: 446, Protein: 26g, Carbohydrates: 6g, Fat: 32g, Fiber: 0g, Cholesterol: 112 mg, Sodium: 1116 mg, Potassium: 104 mg

Directions:

1. Rub the inside of the fondue pot with the cut sides of the garlic clove and discard the garlic.
2. Pour the dry white wine into the fondue pot and cook it over medium heat until it's heated but not boiling.
3. In a separate bowl, toss both the Feta cheese and Gruyère cheese with the cornstarch to coat evenly.
4. Gradually add the cheese mixture to the fondue pot, stirring continuously in a figure-eight pattern to encourage even melting and prevent clumping.
5. Once the cheese has fully melted and the fondue mixture is smooth, stir in the lemon zest, chopped dill, and ouzo (if using). Continue to cook for 2-4 minutes, stirring well.
6. Add a dash of freshly ground black pepper to taste.
7. Reduce the heat to low and serve immediately with an assortment of dippable items, such as crusty bread pieces, fresh vegetables, and grilled meats.

Roasted Garlic and Thyme Fondue

 4 SERVINGS   25 MINUTES   15 MINUTES

Immerse your senses in the savory richness of Roasted Garlic and Thyme Fondue, a delightful combination that enhances the traditional cheese fondue experience with aromatic garlic and earthy thyme. Perfect for a cozy evening, this recipe invites friends and family to gather around the pot, sharing stories and dipping their favorite accompaniments into a silky, cheese-laden indulgence.

Equipment: Fondue pot, Saucepan, Garlic roaster or baking sheet, Cheesecloth

Ingredients:

- 1 Whole head garlic
- 1 1/2 cups Dry white wine
- 1 tbsp Lemon juice
- 1/2 tsp Dijon mustard
- 1/4 tsp Nutmeg, freshly grated
- One tablespoon of freshly chopped fresh thyme leaves, with additional for garnish
- 400g Gruyère cheese, shredded
- 200g Emmentaler cheese, shredded
- 2 tbsp Cornstarch
- Freshly ground black pepper, to taste
- For serving: Cubed crusty bread, steamed vegetables, apples, or other dippers.

Nutritional Information: Calories: 540, Protein: 34g, Carbohydrates: 9g, Fat: 35g, Fiber: 0.2g, Cholesterol: 95 mg, Sodium: 620 mg, Potassium: 200 mg

Directions:

1. Preheat your oven to 200°C (400°F). Cut the top off the garlic head so the cloves are visible, then coat with olive oil and cover with foil. Roast for about 35-40 minutes until caramelized and soft. Once cooled, squeeze cloves from skins and mash into a paste.
2. Rub the inside of the fondue pot with a halved garlic clove for extra flavor if desired, then preheat on medium.
3. In a saucepan, combine the white wine, lemon juice, Dijon mustard, and nutmeg. Over medium heat, bring it to a boil, but watch out not to boil.
4. In a bowl, coat the shredded Gruyère and Emmentaler cheese with cornstarch, ensuring each piece is lightly covered.
5. With a wooden spoon, slowly swirl the cheese into the warm wine mixture in a figure-eight pattern until it melts and becomes creamy. Do not let it boil.
6. Stir in the roasted garlic paste and thyme, and season with freshly ground black pepper.
7. Once the fondue is smooth, transfer it carefully to your prepared fondue pot.
8. Serve immediately with your choice of dippers, sprinkling a little extra thyme over the fondue for garnish.

Broth & Bouillon Fondue Discoveries

Alpine Herb Broth Fondue

 4 SERVINGS   21 MINUTES   30 MINUTES

Discover the savory essence of the Alps with this Alpine Herb Broth Fondue. This fragrant and healthy fondue base is ideal for cooking a variety of meats, seafood, and vegetables, infusing them with the rustic flavors of mountain-grown herbs. Embrace the heartwarming tradition of Swiss fondue with an aromatic twist.

Equipment: Fondue pot, Stove, Cutting board

Ingredients:

- 4 cups Low-sodium beef broth
- 1/2 cup Dry white wine
- 1 Onion, chopped
- 3 Garlic cloves, minced
- 1 Bay leaf
- 1 tsp Dried thyme
- 1 tsp Dried rosemary
- 1/2 tsp Black pepper, freshly ground
- 1/4 tsp Nutmeg, freshly grated
- Assorted dipping foods (cubed beef, chicken, shrimp, mushrooms, and bread)

Nutritional Information: Calories: 50, Protein: 4g, Carbohydrates: 3g, Fat: 0g, Fiber: 0.5g, Cholesterol: 0 mg, Sodium: 150 mg, Potassium: 200 mg

Directions:

1. In a large saucepan, mix together the beef broth, dry white wine, chopped onion, minced garlic, bay leaf, dried thyme, dried rosemary, freshly ground black pepper, and freshly grated nutmeg.
2. To let the flavors meld, bring the mixture to a gentle boil over medium-high heat and then reduce it to a simmer for twenty minutes.
3. After simmering, pour the broth through a fine mesh screen into the fondue pot to remove any solid herbs or onions.
4. Place the fondue pot on its stand over an appropriate heat source to keep the broth hot. Adjust the flame so it gently simmers but does not boil vigorously.
5. Skewer the dipping foods such as cubed beef, chicken, shrimp, mushrooms, and pieces of bread with fondue forks, then cook them in the hot herb broth until done to your liking.
6. Serve the cooked morsels with a variety of dipping sauces on the side, such as garlic aioli, horseradish cream, or Dijon mustard sauce.

Asian Spice Market Fondue

 8 SERVINGS   21 MINUTES   30 MINUTES

Immerse yourself in an aromatic journey with this Asian Spice Market Fondue, a fragrant broth fondue that combines the warmth of spices and the richness of a savory broth. Perfect for dipping an assortment of meats and vegetables, it is a fondue that celebrates the diverse flavors of the Asian spice bazaars.

Equipment: Fondue pot, Burner, Skewers or fondue forks

Ingredients:

- 4 cups Beef broth (preferably low-sodium)
- 1 cup Shaoxing wine (Chinese cooking wine)
- 2 Star anise
- 1 Cinnamon stick
- 4 slices Fresh ginger
- 3 cloves Garlic, smashed
- 1 tbsp Sichuan peppercorns
- 2 tsp Soy sauce
- 1 tsp Fish sauce
- 1 tsp Brown sugar
- 1 Green onion, chopped for garnish
- 1 Fresh red chili, thinly sliced for garnish

Nutritional Information: Calories: 68, Protein: 4g, Carbohydrates: 5g, Fat: 0g, Fiber: 0.4g, Cholesterol: 0 mg, Sodium: 870 mg, Potassium: 150 mg

Directions:

1. Heat the beef broth in the fondue pot over medium heat until it simmers.
2. Stir in the Shaoxing wine.
3. Add star anise, cinnamon stick, ginger slices, and smashed garlic cloves to infuse the broth with their flavors.
4. Add Sichuan peppercorns for a numbing sensation.
5. Mix in soy sauce and fish sauce for umami depth, and a pinch of brown sugar to balance the flavors.
6. Simmer gently for 30 minutes to thoroughly infuse the spices.
7. Skim off any impurities from the surface before serving.
8. Garnish with chopped green onions and red chili slices for a vibrant finish.
9. Keep the broth at a medium simmer for dipping thinly sliced meats, mushrooms, tofu, or vegetables with skewers or fondue forks.
10. Serve with side sauces like hoisin, sriracha, or sesame oil for enhanced flavor and dipping.

Savory Garlic Chicken Broth Fondue

 4 SERVINGS 16 MINUTES 20 MINUTES

Discover the comforting depths of a savory garlic chicken broth as a delicious base for your next fondue experience. This aromatic broth is perfect for dipping vegetables, meats, and even some breads, turning each dip into an explosion of layered flavors that enhance your fondue ingredients.

Equipment: Fondue pot, Stove, Measuring cups and spoons

Ingredients:

- 4 cups Chicken broth, low-sodium
- 1 cup Dry white wine
- 4 cloves Garlic, minced
- 1 medium Onion, finely chopped
- 1 tsp Dried thyme
- 1 tsp Black peppercorns
- 2 Bay leaves
- 1 tbsp Soy sauce
- 2 tbsp Fresh parsley, chopped
- Selection of dip-ables (chicken breast cubes, shrimp, thinly sliced beef, mushrooms, bread cubes, etc.)

Nutritional Information: Calories: 65 (excluding dip-ables), Protein: 2g, Carbohydrates: 3g, Fat: 0g, Fiber: 0.2g, Cholesterol: 0 mg, Sodium: 570 mg, Potassium: 61 mg

Directions:

1. Heat the chicken broth, white wine, dried thyme, black peppercorns, bay leaves, and garlic and onion in a big pot.
2. Bring to a simmer and cook for about 10 minutes to enable the flavors to combine. Stir the mixture occasionally. Stir occasionally.
3. Add soy sauce to the simmering broth for added depth of flavor.
4. Carefully strain the mixture to remove solids, and return the liquid back to the pot to keep warm.
5. Transfer the hot prepared broth to your fondue pot over the lowest possible flame to maintain a gentle simmer.
6. Skewer your chosen dip-ables with fondue forks and cook them in the hot broth until they reach your desired doneness.
7. Using a slotted spoon, sprinkle fresh parsley into the broth and give a gentle stir.
8. Invite guests to start dipping and enjoying immediately.

Mediterranean Seafood Saffron Broth

 6 SERVINGS 15 MINUTES 25 MINUTES

With this Seafood Saffron Broth, you can immerse yourself in the rich tastes of the Mediterranean while enjoying an exquisite fondue. Perfectly balanced with aromatic spices, seafood, and a hint of saffron, this broth is a delightful way to cook and savor your favorite seafood, delivering a luxurious taste of coastal cuisine right at your dinner table.

Equipment: Large pot, Fondue set, Ladle

Ingredients:

- 8 cups Fish or vegetable stock
- 1 pinch Saffron threads
- 1/2 cup Dry white wine
- 2 cloves Garlic, minced
- 1 small Onion, diced
- 1 Lemon, zest and juice
- 1 teaspoon Paprika
- 1/2 teaspoon Red pepper flakes (optional)
- 1 tablespoon Olive oil
- Freshly ground black pepper, to taste
- Salt, to taste
- Assorted fresh seafood (shrimp, scallops, firm white fish, mussels), prepared for fondue
- Fresh herbs (e.g., parsley and dill) for garnish.

Nutritional Information: Calories: 180, Protein: 24g, Carbohydrates: 6g, Fat: 4g, Fiber: 0.5g, Cholesterol: 85 mg, Sodium: 870 mg, Potassium: 360 mg

Directions:

1. In a large pot, preheat the olive oil over medium heat. Sauté the minced garlic and diced onion until they are transparent and aromatic.
2. Stir in paprika, red pepper flakes (if using), and a pinch of saffron threads. Toast the spices briefly to release their flavors.
3. Pour in the dry white wine and boil for 2-3 minutes, or until slightly reduced.
4. Add the fish or vegetable stock and bring the mixture to a gentle simmer. Lemon zest and juice are added, then salt and freshly ground black pepper are added to taste.
5. Keep the broth at a moderate simmer for about 15 minutes to enable the flavors to combine. Adjust seasoning as needed.
6. Once the broth is ready, transfer it to the fondue pot set over a flame that keeps the broth at a gentle simmer.
7. Skewer your choice of seafood and submerge in the simmering broth, cooking each piece until it's done to your preference.
8. If you'd like, serve the cooked fish with your preferred dipping sauces and garnish it with fresh herbs.

Caribbean Coconut Curry Fondue

 4 SERVINGS   25 MINUTES   30 MINUTES

Immerse your taste buds in the tropical flavors of the Caribbean with this Coconut Curry Fondue. A creamy blend of coconut milk and aromatic spices forms the perfect bath to dip a variety of fresh seafood and crisp vegetables. This comforting and exotic fondue brings a smoky sweetness to your table, sure to transport your guests to an island paradise with every bite.

Equipment: Fondue pot, Stove, Whisk

Ingredients:

- 1 can (13.5 oz) Unsweetened coconut milk
- 2 cups Seafood or vegetable broth
- 3 tbsp Curry powder
- 1 tbsp Brown sugar
- 1 tsp Garlic, minced
- 1 tsp Ginger, freshly grated
- 1/2 tsp Turmeric powder
- 1/4 tsp cayenne (adjust according to taste)
- Salt and pepper to taste
- Assorted dippers: Shrimp (peeled & deveined), scallops, bell peppers, mushrooms, broccoli florets, etc.

Nutritional Information: Calories: 250, Protein: 5g, Carbohydrates: 15g, Fat: 20g, Fiber: 2g, Cholesterol: 0 mg, Sodium: 500 mg, Potassium: 260 mg

Directions:

1. Begin by pre-warming your fondue pot on a medium heat setting on the stove.
2. Stir together the seafood or vegetable broth and coconut milk after adding them to the pot.
3. Add the curry powder, brown sugar, minced garlic, and grated ginger into the coconut milk mixture while continuously whisking to ensure there are no lumps.
4. Sprinkle in the turmeric, cayenne pepper, and season with salt and pepper to your liking. After bringing the mixture to a gentle simmer, cook it for about ten minutes, whisking once and again. This will enable the tastes to meld and become more intense.
5. Carefully transfer the fondue pot to its stand over a flame or onto a warming surface, if not already situated.
6. With fondue forks or skewers, guests can dip their chosen seafood and vegetables into the aromatic Caribbean coconut curry, allowing them to cook gently and absorb the flavors.
7. Cook seafood until opaque and vegetables until tender but still crisp, usually a couple of minutes for each dip.

Tuscan Tomato Basil Broth Fondue

 4 SERVINGS   15 MINUTES   30 MINUTES

Dive into the heart of Italy with this Tuscan Tomato Basil Broth Fondue, a perfect blend of ripe tomatoes, fresh basil, and rich Italian herbs. This light and fragrant broth creates a sophisticated flavor base that pairs wonderfully with a variety of dippable delights, offering a refreshing alternative to the traditional cheese or chocolate fondue.

Equipment: Fondue pot, stove, cutting board, chef's knife, measuring cups and spoons

Ingredients:

- 4 cups Vegetable broth
- 2 cups Ripe tomatoes, diced
- 1/2 cup Dry white wine
- 1/4 cup Fresh basil leaves, chiffonade
- 2 cloves Garlic, minced
- 1 tbsp Olive oil
- 1 tsp Italian seasoning
- For an extra spicy kick, add 1/2 tsp of red pepper flakes.
- Add freshly ground black pepper and salt to taste.

Nutritional Information: Calories: 85, Protein: 2g, Carbohydrates: 9g, Fat: 3g, Fiber: 2g, Cholesterol: 0 mg, Sodium: 200 mg, Potassium: 360 mg

Directions:

1. In a medium saucepan, heat the olive oil over medium heat. When the garlic is aromatic, add the minced garlic and boil for one minute.
2. Add the diced tomatoes and cook for another 5-7 minutes, until the tomatoes have softened and released their juices.
3. After adding the dry white wine and vegetable broth, boil the mixture.
4. Stir in the Italian seasoning, red pepper flakes (if using), and fresh basil. Season with salt and freshly ground pepper to taste. In order to give the flavors time to combine, lower the heat and boil the soup for 20 minutes.
5. Once the broth is ready, transfer it carefully into a preheated fondue pot set on a burner to keep the broth warm for dipping.
6. Skewer your desired dippables, such as cubes of crusty bread, blanched vegetables, or your choice of protein, and then carefully cook them in the hot broth until done to your liking.

French Countryside Wine Broth Fondue

 4 SERVINGS 21 MINUTES 30 MINUTES

Escape to the rolling hills of the French countryside with each savory dip into this wine broth fondue. Infused with the flavors of rich Burgundy wine, fresh herbs, and aromatic vegetables, this fondue broth is perfect for tenderly cooking your favorite meats and vegetables, offering an elegant and interactive dining experience.

Equipment: Fondue pot, Cutting board, Knife

Ingredients:

- 750 ml Burgundy wine
- 2 cups beef broth
- 1 medium onion, thinly sliced
- 4 cloves garlic, minced
- 1 bouquet garni (thyme, parsley, and bay leaf tied together)
- 1 tsp whole black peppercorns
- 1/2 tsp salt
- Assorted dipping ingredients such as cubed beef tenderloin, chicken breast, shrimp, small potatoes, and mushrooms

Nutritional Information: Calories: 220, Protein: 3g, Carbohydrates: 8g, Fat: 0g, Fiber: 1g, Cholesterol: 0 mg, Sodium: 570 mg, Potassium: 380 mg

Directions:

1. Combine the Burgundy wine and beef broth in the fondue pot and turn on the heat to bring the mixture to a simmer.
2. As the wine and broth begin to warm, add minced garlic and the thinly sliced onion to the pot, allowing them to infuse the broth with flavor.
3. Gently place the bouquet garni into the broth along with the black peppercorns and salt.
4. Allow the broth to simmer gently for 15-20 minutes so the flavors from the herbs, onion, and garlic become well combined with the wine and beef broth.
5. Once the broth is fragrant and flavorful, adjust the fondue burner to maintain a steady simmer suitable for cooking the dipping ingredients.
6. Spear your choice of meat or vegetables with fondue forks and cook in the simmering broth until it reaches the desired level of doneness.
7. Serve with an assortment of dipping sauces on the side to complement the flavors of the cooked ingredients.

Moroccan Lemon & Olive Broth Fondue

 4 SERVINGS 20 MINUTES 30 MINUTES

Immerse your senses in the exotic flavors of Morocco with this fragrant Lemon & Olive Broth Fondue. Aromatic spices and zesty lemon blend with green olives to create a broth that is both tangy and savory, perfect for dipping a variety of meats, vegetables, and bread. This broth's unique blend of tastes will take you to the vibrant souks of Marrakech, making your fondue experience a gourmet journey.

Equipment: Fondue pot, Cutting board, Chef's knife

Ingredients:

- 4 cups beef or chicken broth
- Zest of 1 lemon
- Juice of 1 lemon
- 1/2 cup pitted green olives, sliced
- 1 teaspoon ground cumin
- 1/2 teaspoon ground coriander
- 1/2 teaspoon paprika
- 1/4 teaspoon ground cinnamon
- 1/4 teaspoon cayenne pepper (optional for heat)
- 2 tablespoons fresh cilantro, chopped
- 1 tablespoon olive oil
- Salt and pepper to taste

Nutritional Information: Calories: 84, Protein: 6g, Carbohydrates: 4g, Fat: 5g, Fiber: 1g, Cholesterol: 0 mg, Sodium: 879 mg, Potassium: 199 mg

Directions:

1. Add the olive oil to a big saucepan and place it over medium heat. Once hot, add the spices (cumin, coriander, paprika, cinnamon, and cayenne pepper) and toast them for about 2 minutes until fragrant.
2. Pour the broth into the saucepan and increase the heat to bring the mixture to a simmer. Add the lemon zest, lemon juice, and sliced green olives to the broth.
3. Allow the broth to simmer gently for 15-20 minutes so that the flavors meld together. Season with salt and pepper to taste.
4. Once the broth is seasoned and aromatic, pour it into the fondue pot. Set up the fondue pot on its stand over the burner to keep the broth warm.
5. Arrange meats, vegetables, and bread for dipping around the fondue pot.
6. Skewer the dipping ingredients with fondue forks and cook them in the hot broth until done to your liking. Sprinkle fresh cilantro over the fondue before serving for an extra pop of flavor.

Bavarian Beer Broth Fondue

 4 SERVINGS 15 MINUTES 30 MINUTES

Infuse the spirit of Bavaria into your fondue night with this robust and flavorful Bavarian Beer Broth Fondue. A golden, hoppy broth becomes the fondue base, perfect for dunking an array of meats, vegetables, and breads. It's a hearty twist on traditional fondue that beer enthusiast and fondue lovers alike will relish.

Equipment: Fondue Pot, Stove, Cutting Board, Knife

Ingredients:

- 24 oz Bavarian-style beer (such as Weißbier)
- 4 cups beef stock
- 2 cloves garlic, minced
- 1 yellow onion, diced
- 1 tbsp whole grain mustard
- 2 bay leaves
- 1 tsp dried thyme
- ½ tsp black pepper, freshly ground
- 1 tbsp Worcestershire sauce
- Assortment of fondue dippers: cubed beef, sliced bratwurst, mushrooms, cherry tomatoes, broccoli florets, and crusty bread

Nutritional Information: Calories: 150, Protein: 10g, Carbohydrates: 12g, Fat: 1g, Fiber: 0.5g, Cholesterol: 0 mg, Sodium: 320 mg, Potassium: 85 mg

Directions:

1. Simmer the mixture for a another 10 minutes or so to enhance the complexity of flavor.
2. Stir in the minced garlic, diced onion, whole grain mustard, bay leaves, dried thyme, and black pepper, blending all the flavors together.
3. Simmer the mixture for a another 10 minutes or so to enhance the complexity of flavor.
4. Add the Worcestershire sauce and continue simmering the broth for another 20 minutes on low heat. This will concentrate the flavors further, infusing the broth with a deep umami taste.
5. Once done, remove the bay leaves and arrange your array of fondue dippers alongside the pot.
6. Skewer your chosen dippers and submerge them into the hot broth, cooking them to your desired doneness.
7. Serve immediately, allowing guests to cook and season their selections right at the table.

Pacific Rim Ginger Broth Fondue

 6 SERVINGS 16 MINUTES 30 MINUTES

Explore the flavors of the Pacific Rim with this aromatic ginger broth fondue, which provides a savory and health-conscious base perfect for dipping your favorite seafood, vegetables, and meats. The zesty ginger paired with the umami of soy and the freshness of cilantro creates an experience that's both invigorating and comforting.

Equipment: Fondue pot, Stove, Knife, Cutting board

Ingredients:

- 6 cups Chicken or Vegetable Stock
- 1/4 cup Soy Sauce
- Three tablespoons of freshly peeled and finely sliced ginger
- 2 Garlic Cloves, minced
- Two Green Onions, thinly sliced plus more for garnish
- 1 Fresh Red Chili, thinly sliced (seeds removed for less heat, if desired)
- 1 Lemongrass Stalk, tough outer leaves removed, lightly smashed and cut into 2-inch pieces
- 1/4 cup chopped fresh cilantro and more for garnish
- 1 tablespoon Sesame Oil
- 2 tablespoons Mirin or Dry Sherry (optional)
- Dipping Ingredients of Choice (thinly sliced beef, shrimp, tofu, mushrooms, bok choy, etc.)

Nutritional Information: Calories: 70, Protein: 4g, Carbohydrates: 4g, Fat: 4g, Fiber: 0g, Cholesterol: 0 mg, Sodium: 1200 mg, Potassium: 80 mg

Directions:

1. Stir together the soy sauce, ginger, garlic, green onions, red chile, and lemongrass in a large saucepan with the chicken or vegetable stock. Simmer the mixture for a moderate amount of time over medium heat.
2. Simmer the soup for 21 minutes to allow the flavors of the aromatics to seep in.
3. While the broth is simmering, prepare your dipping ingredients by cutting them into bite-sized pieces and arranging them on a platter.
4. After 20 minutes, strain the broth to remove the aromatics, then return the liquid to the pot. Stir in the cilantro, sesame oil, and mirin or dry sherry if using, and continue to simmer for an additional 10 minutes.
5. Carefully transfer the hot broth to your fondue pot and set it on its stand over a burner to keep warm.
6. Spear your chosen dipping ingredients with fondue forks and submerge them into the hot broth to cook to your desired doneness.
7. Garnish the served broth with additional thinly sliced green onions and fresh cilantro.

Argentine Chimichurri Beef Broth Fondue

 6 SERVINGS   20 MINUTES   90 MINUTES

Savor the bold flavors of Argentina with this herby and vibrant chimichurri beef broth fondue. Perfect for a meat-lovers' gathering, this recipe combines the zest of chimichurri with a rich beef broth for dipping your favorite fondue ingredients.

Equipment: Fondue pot, Mixing bowl, Cutting board, Knife

Ingredients:

- 6 cups Beef broth
- One pound of tender beef, sliced into 1-inch pieces
- 1/2 cup Fresh parsley, finely chopped
- 1/4 cup Fresh oregano, finely chopped
- 4 cloves Garlic, minced
- 2 tbsp Red wine vinegar
- 1/2 cup Olive oil
- 1 tsp Crushed red pepper flakes
- 1 tsp Salt
- 1/2 tsp Black pepper, freshly ground
- Assorted vegetables (like bell peppers, mushrooms, and onions) and bread cubes for dipping

Nutritional Information: Calories: 320, Protein: 24g, Carbohydrates: 4g, Fat: 24g, Fiber: 1g, Cholesterol: 75 mg, Sodium: 820 mg, Potassium: 360 mg

Directions:

1. To make the chimichurri sauce, garlic, combine parsley, olive oil, oregano, red wine vinegar, salt, crushed red pepper flakes, and black pepper in a mixing bowl. Blend thoroughly and let to let the flavors blend.
2. Pour beef broth into the fondue pot and bring to a simmer over medium heat. The beef should be cooked but not overcooked in the soup.
3. Stir half of the chimichurri sauce into the simmering beef broth, reserving the rest for dipping or drizzling.
4. Place the beef tenderloin cubes on fondue forks or skewers. Dip and cook each piece of beef in the chimichurri beef broth until it reaches the desired level of doneness, usually about 2 to 3 minutes for medium-rare.
5. Serve immediately with the reserved chimichurri sauce, assorted vegetables, and bread cubes for dipping and cooking in the broth.
6. Guests can cook their own beef and vegetables in the simmering broth and use the remaining chimichurri sauce as a condiment.

Thai Coconut Lemongrass Fondue

 4 SERVINGS   20 MINUTES   30 MINUTES

This Thai Coconut Lemongrass Fondue infuses the rich flavors of Southeast Asia into a warming, communal meal. Aromatic lemongrass, creamy coconut milk, and a touch of heat from fresh ginger and chili create a broth that's perfect for dipping an array of meats, seafood, and vegetables. It's a delightful twist on traditional fondue that brings a taste of Thailand to your table.

Equipment: Fondue pot, Chafing dish, Skewers or fondue forks

Ingredients:

- 2 cans (13.5 ounces each) Coconut milk
- 2 cups Chicken or vegetable broth
- 2 stalks Lemongrass, tough outer layers removed, cut into 3-inch pieces and bruised
- One inch of freshly peeled and thinly sliced ginger
- 2 Garlic cloves, peeled and smashed
- 1 Small red chili, deseeded and finely chopped
- 1 tbsp Brown sugar
- 2 tbsp Fish sauce, or to taste
- 2 tbsp Lime juice
- 1 bunch Fresh cilantro, coarsely chopped
- 1 tsp Salt, or to taste
- Freshly ground black pepper, to taste
- Assorted dipping ingredients such as sliced chicken, beef, shrimp, mushrooms, and bell peppers

Nutritional Information: Calories: 290, Protein: 3g, Carbohydrates: 7g, Fat: 28g, Fiber: 0g, Cholesterol: 0 mg, Sodium: 1750 mg, Potassium: 200 mg

Directions:

1. Combine the coconut milk with the chicken or vegetable broth in your fondue pot or chafing dish, and heat it gently over medium heat.
2. Add the bruised lemongrass stalks, sliced ginger, smashed garlic, and chopped red chili to the liquid, and simmer for 5 minutes to allow the flavors to infuse into the broth.
3. Stir in brown sugar, fish sauce, and lime juice. To get the right amount of acidity or saltiness, add more lime juice or fish sauce.
4. Add in half of the chopped cilantro, reserving the rest for garnish. When seasoning, add salt and freshly ground black pepper to taste. Let the broth simmer for an additional 10 minutes on low heat, stirring occasionally.
5. Arrange the raw dipping ingredients on a platter around the fondue pot. Skewer the items and cook them in the simmering broth until done to the desired level. Typically, thin slices of meat will cook in 2-3 minutes, while vegetables may vary depending on type and size.
6. Garnish the broth with the remaining fresh cilantro just before serving.

Vietnamese Pho Broth Fondue

 6 SERVINGS 31 MINUTES 120 MINUTES

Delve into the aromatic world of Vietnamese cuisine with this Pho Broth Fondue – a twist that turns traditional pho into a communal fondue feast. The rich, fragrant broth serves as the perfect simmering base for cooking thin slices of meat, seafood, and vegetables, infusing them with the spices and flavors reminiscent of the streets of Hanoi.

Equipment: Fondue pot, Burner, Ladle, Skewers or Fondue forks

Ingredients:

- 2 quarts Beef stock; 1 large Onion, charred
- 4-inch piece Ginger, charred and sliced
- 3 Star anise; 4 Cloves
- 1 Cinnamon stick; 2 Cardamom pods
- 1 tsp Coriander seeds; 2 tbsp Fish sauce
- 1 tbsp Brown sugar
- 1-2 Thai chiles, sliced (optional for heat)
- Salt, to taste; Fresh cilantro, chopped (for garnish)
- Fresh basil, chopped (for garnish)
- Bean sprouts (for serving); Lime wedges (for serving)
- Thinly sliced beef, chicken, or seafood (for dipping)
- Assorted vegetables (such as bok choy, mushrooms, or bell peppers), sliced (for dipping)

Nutritional Information: Calories: 210, Protein: 30g, Carbohydrates: 10g, Fat: 4g, Fiber: 1g, Cholesterol: 60 mg, Sodium: 800 mg, Potassium: 400 mg

Directions:

1. Char the onion and ginger in a big pot under a broiler or over an open flame until the outsides are nicely browned. This will add depth to your broth.
2. Pour the beef stock into the fondue pot and place it on the stovetop over medium heat, just simmering.
3. Add the charred onion, sliced ginger, star anise, cloves, cinnamon stick, cardamom pods, and coriander seeds to the broth.
4. Let the flavors infiltrate by simmering the broth for a minimum of one hour. For a deeper flavor, simmer for up to 2 hours, occasionally skimming off any impurities that rise to the top.
5. Add the brown sugar, fish sauce, Thai chilies (if using), and salt to taste.
6. Strain the aromatics from the broth, then return the clear broth to the fondue pot.
7. Place the fondue pot on its burner set to a low heat to maintain a gentle simmer.
8. Arrange the meat, seafood, vegetables, garnishes, and dipping sauces around the fondue pot.
9. Using fondue forks or skewers, guests can cook their own selection of meats and vegetables in the simmering broth.
10. Add some cilantro and basil for garnish, and serve with bean sprouts and lime wedges on the side for some extra crunch and acidity.

Indian Spice Infusion Fondue

 6 SERVINGS 15 MINUTES 30 MINUTES

Dive into the aromatic world of Indian cuisine with this Indian Spice Infusion Fondue. The fragrant blend of spices will transport you to the bustling streets of India, as this innovative fondue fuses traditional Indian flavors into a delightful broth perfect for dipping and savoring. Ideal for those looking to adventure into new culinary territories and awaken their palates with warmth and exotic taste.

Equipment: Fondue pot, Measuring spoons, Chopping board, Knife

Ingredients:

- 6 cups Chicken or vegetable broth
- 1 Cinnamon stick
- 3 Cardamom pods, slightly crushed
- 4 Cloves
- 2 Star anise
- 2 tsp Cumin seeds
- 1 tsp Coriander seeds
- 1 inch Ginger, freshly grated
- 2 Garlic cloves, minced
- 1 tbsp Ghee (or unsalted butter)
- 1/4 tsp Ground turmeric
- 1 tsp Garam masala
- Salt to taste
- Assorted vegetables (like bell peppers, mushrooms, zucchini), meats, or seafood for dipping

Nutritional Information: Calories: 35, Protein: 1g, Carbohydrates: 2g, Fat: 2.5g, Fiber: 0.5g, Cholesterol: 10 mg, Sodium: 950 mg, Potassium: 30 mg

Directions:

1. In a medium-sized pan, dry roast the cumin seeds, coriander seeds, cardamom pods, cloves, and star anise over medium heat until aromatic, about 1-2 minutes. Be careful not to burn the spices.
2. Using the same pan, melt the ghee over medium heat and sauté the ginger and garlic until golden and fragrant, around 2 minutes.
3. Transfer the toasted spices, sautéed ginger, and garlic into the fondue pot. Add the chicken or vegetable broth, cinnamon stick, ground turmeric, and garam masala.
4. To let the tastes of the spices seep into the broth, bring the mixture to a moderate boil, then lower the heat and simmer for 20 minutes.
5. Remove the entire spices from the broth by straining it, then transfer the liquid back to the fondue pot and keep it heated. You may leave some finer spices in for added texture and flavor if desired.
6. Adjust the seasoning with salt to taste and ensure the broth is hot before serving.
7. Serve with a platter of vegetables, meats, or seafood to dip into the spicy, flavored broth with fondue forks or skewers.

Italian Parmesan Brodo Fondue

 4 SERVINGS   15 MINUTES   30 MINUTES

Indulge in the rich umami flavor of Italian Parmesan Brodo Fondue. This delightful fusion of a classic broth with the bold taste of Parmigiano-Reggiano is perfect for dipping your favorite meats and vegetables, offering a comforting and sophisticated take on fondue.

Equipment: Fondue pot, Stove, Whisk

Ingredients:

- 4 cups beef or chicken broth
- 1 cup dry white wine
- 1 clove garlic, halved
- 2 cups Parmigiano-Reggiano cheese, freshly grated
- 2 tablespoons cornstarch
- Salt and pepper to taste
- Optional dippers: cubes of crusty Italian bread, vegetables (mushrooms, asparagus, bell peppers), or thinly sliced meats (beef, chicken, or shrimp)

Nutritional Information: Calories: 230, Protein: 19g, Carbohydrates: 4g, Fat: 12g, Fiber: 0g, Cholesterol: 30 mg, Sodium: 690 mg, Potassium: 50 mg

Directions:

1. Heat the white wine and broth in a medium saucepan until they are gently simmering. Add the halved garlic clove to infuse the liquid with its flavor for about 5 minutes.
2. Meanwhile, toss the grated Parmigiano-Reggiano with the cornstarch in a separate bowl to coat the cheese evenly. This will help prevent clumping when added to the broth.
3. Take out and discard the garlic from the broth. In order to make a smooth fondue, gradually add the cheese mixture to the simmering stock while stirring continuously.
4. Continue whisking until the broth has slightly thickened and the cheese has melted completely, creating a rich, creamy consistency.
5. Season the Parmesan Brodo with a pinch of salt and pepper to taste.
6. Carefully transfer the broth into your fondue pot set over a low flame to keep warm.
7. Serve with your choice of dippers arranged around the fondue pot. Use fondue forks or skewers to dip the items into the hot cheesy broth mixture.
8. Stir the fondue from time to time to prevent any cheese from settling at the bottom.

Mexican Fiesta Broth Fondue

 6 SERVINGS   30 MINUTES   60 MINUTES

This Mexican Fiesta Broth Fondue is a lively and aromatic blend of bold Mexican flavors that makes for a perfect interactive dining experience. The rich, savory broth serves as a flavorful medium for cooking a variety of meats and vegetables, turning each bite into a fiesta of taste.

Equipment: Fondue pot, Burner or stove, Ladle, Skewers or fondue forks

Ingredients:

- 6 cups beef or chicken broth
- 1 medium onion, finely chopped
- 2 cloves garlic, minced
- 1 jalapeño, seeded and finely chopped
- 1 cup crushed tomatoes
- 1/2 cup fresh cilantro leaves, chopped
- 1 tsp cumin; 1/2 tsp chili powder
- 1/2 tsp smoked paprika
- Salt and pepper to taste
- 1 lime, juiced
- 1 lb chicken breast, cubed (for dipping)
- 1 lb beef sirloin, cubed (for dipping)
- Assorted vegetables (bell peppers, mushrooms, cherry tomatoes), prepped for dipping
- Tortilla strips, for garnish

Directions:

1. Add the broth, onion, garlic, jalapeño, crushed tomatoes, cilantro, cumin, chili powder, smoked paprika, and a dash of salt and pepper to a large saucepan set over medium heat. Simmer the mixture for a while.
2. Cook for about 31 minutes, partially covered, stirring occasionally to blend the flavors together.
3. Add the lime juice, adjust seasonings if necessary, and then transfer the broth into a fondue pot set over a flame to keep it at a gentle simmer.
4. Skewer a cube of chicken or beef or your choice of vegetables, and submerge in the hot broth to cook to desired doneness. Typically, meats will take 2-5 minutes to cook through.
5. Garnish with crispy tortilla strips for an added crunch and to embrace the Mexican cuisine theme.

Nutritional Information: Calories: 50, Protein: 4g, Carbohydrates: 5g, Fat: 1g, Fiber: 1g, Cholesterol: 0 mg, Sodium: 800 mg, Potassium: 200 mg"

Nordic Dill & Juniper Broth Fondue

 6 SERVINGS   15 MINUTES   30 MINUTES

This Nordic Dill & Juniper Broth Fondue is an aromatic journey into Scandinavian cuisine, featuring the fresh, herbal notes of dill and the crisp, peppery essence of juniper berries. It's a light and invigorating twist on traditional fondue that pairs beautifully with seafood and root vegetables.

Equipment: Fondue pot, Stovetop, Cheesecloth or fine sieve

Ingredients:

- 6 cups Beef or vegetable broth
- 1/2 cup Dry white wine
- 3 tbsp Fresh dill, chopped, plus extra for garnish
- 1 tbsp Juniper berries, lightly crushed
- 2 tbsp Shallots, finely chopped
- 2 cloves Garlic, minced
- 1 tsp Whole black peppercorns
- 1 tbsp Olive oil
- 1 tsp Sea salt, or to taste
- Optional dippers: Boiled baby potatoes, roasted root vegetables, crusty bread, cooked shrimp, or sliced chicken.

Nutritional Information: Calories: 75, Protein: 5g, Carbohydrates: 4g, Fat: 3g, Fiber: 1g, Cholesterol: 0 mg, Sodium: 780 mg, Potassium: 150 mg

Directions:

1. Heat the olive oil in a large saucepan over medium heat. Cook the garlic and shallots for two to three minutes, or until translucent.
2. To deglaze the pan, add the dry white wine and use a wooden spoon to scrape out any brown pieces.
3. Pour in the vegetable or beef broth and heat to a gentle boil.
4. Add the sea salt, fresh dill, whole black peppercorns, and crushed juniper berries, then lower the heat to a simmer. Cover and allow the broth to infuse for about 15-20 minutes.
5. While the broth simmers, prepare your dippers and arrange them on serving plates.
6. After the broth has infused, pour it through a cheesecloth or fine sieve into the fondue pot to remove the solid herbs and spices.
7. Place the fondue pot on its stand over a burner at the table and adjust the flame to maintain a gentle simmer.
8. Spear the dippers with fondue forks and simmer them in the broth until cooked to your liking.
9. Garnish the fondue broth with additional fresh dill if desired.

New England Seafood Broth Fondue

 6 SERVINGS   21 MINUTES   30 MINUTES

Indulge in the essence of coastal New England with this savory seafood broth fondue. This fondue is ideal for seafood enthusiasts, with a rich blend of herbs and ocean flavors that will make your taste buds dance with ecstasy, putting a unique spin on the typical broth fondue.

Equipment: Fondue Pot, Stovetop, Ladle

Ingredients:

- 8 cups Fish stock or seafood broth
- 1 cup Dry white wine
- 1/2 cup Onion, finely chopped
- 3 Cloves garlic, minced
- 1 Bay leaf
- 1 tsp Thyme, dried
- 1/2 tsp Black pepper, freshly ground
- 3 tbsp Fresh parsley, chopped
- 2 tbsp Lemon juice
- 1 tbsp Old Bay seasoning
- 1 lb Assorted seafood (shrimp, scallops, small pieces of firm fish like cod)
- Additional vegetables and dipping items (baby potatoes, mushrooms, cherry tomatoes)

Nutritional Information: Calories: 215, Protein: 26g, Carbohydrates: 8g, Fat: 4g, Fiber: 1g, Cholesterol: 85 mg, Sodium: 705 mg, Potassium: 468 mg

Directions:

1. In a large saucepan, combine fish stock or seafood broth with dry white wine, bring to a simmer over medium heat.
2. Add the finely chopped onion and garlic, and cook for 5 minutes, or until the onions are transparent.
3. Introduce bay leaf, thyme, black pepper, and Old Bay seasoning to the simmering stock.
4. Continue to boil slowly for another 15 minutes, allowing the flavors to combine.
5. As the broth simmers, prepare the seafood and vegetables by rinsing them and cutting them into bite-sized pieces if necessary.
6. Strain the broth to remove the solid pieces, then return it to the pot. Add the fresh parsley and lemon juice for an extra flavor boost.
7. If using an electric fondue pot, pour the broth into the pot and adjust the temperature to maintain a gentle simmer. For a traditional fondue pot, keep the broth heated on the stove until ready to serve, then transfer to a fondue pot with an adjustable flame.
8. Skewer pieces of seafood and vegetables with fondue forks and cook them in the simmering broth until seafood is cooked through and the vegetables are tender.
9. Serve with crusty bread, assorted dipping sauces such as tartar sauce, remoulade, or cocktail sauce, and enjoy a truly maritime dining experience.

Provencal Herb de Provence Broth Fondue

 6 SERVINGS 20 MINUTES 30 MINUTES

The Provencal Herb de Provence Broth Fondue brings the fragrant scents and tastes of Southern France to your table, perfect for a rustic and aromatic dipping experience. Rich with herbs and a gentle simmering broth, it's sure to delight the senses and offer a unique twist to your fondue repertoire.

Equipment: Fondue pot, Burner, Ladle

Ingredients:

- 6 cups Beef or vegetable broth
- 1 cup Dry white wine
- 3 cloves Garlic, minced
- 1 medium Onion, finely chopped
- 2 tbsp Herbes de Provence
- 1 tsp Black peppercorns
- 1 Bay leaf
- 1/2 tsp Salt, or to taste
- 1 tbsp Olive oil
- Assorted dipping ingredients such as cubed beef, chicken, seafood, or vegetables

Nutritional Information: Calories: 70, Protein: 2g, Carbohydrates: 3g, Fat: 2g, Fiber: 0g, Cholesterol: 0 mg, Sodium: 1300 mg, Potassium: 100 mg

Directions:

1. Heat the olive oil in a big saucepan over medium heat. Sauté the chopped onion and minced garlic until translucent and fragrant, about 3-5 minutes.
2. After adding the dry white wine, let it boil for three minutes or so, until it reduces significantly.
3. Black peppercorns, bay leaf, salt, and Herbes de Provence should all be added to the pot along with the beef or veggie broth. Mix thoroughly to blend the ingredients.
4. Bring the mixture to a gentle boil, then reduce the heat, cover, and let it simmer for about 20 minutes to infuse the broth with the flavors of the herbs and seasoning.
5. Strain the broth to remove the solid herbs and peppercorns, if desired, for a clearer liquid. Then, transfer the strained broth into your fondue pot, which you should place on its burner to keep warm.
6. Adjust the fondue burner to maintain the broth at a gentle simmer for dipping and cooking your chosen ingredients.

Szechuan Spicy Broth Fondue

 6 SERVINGS 15 MINUTES 30 MINUTES

Immerse your fondue night into the depths of spicy Szechuan cuisine with this piquant broth fondue. This flavorful concoction combines the aromatic heat of Szechuan peppercorns with a medley of Chinese spices, offering a sizzling fondue experience that pairs perfectly with a variety of dippable delights like thinly sliced meats, mushrooms, and tofu.

Equipment: Fondue pot, Stove, Ladle

Ingredients:

- 6 cups Beef or chicken broth
- 2 tbsp Szechuan peppercorns
- 2 Star anise
- 1 Cinnamon stick
- 2 tbsp Chili bean sauce (Doubanjiang)
- 1 tbsp Soy sauce
- 2 tsp Sesame oil
- 3 slices Ginger, fresh
- 3 cloves Garlic, smashed
- 2 Green onions, roughly chopped
- 1 tsp Sugar
- 2 tbsp Chinese cooking wine (Shaoxing wine)
- 1/4 tsp Ground white pepper
- Fresh vegetables, meats, and tofu for dipping

Nutritional Information: Calories: 98, Protein: 5g, Carbohydrates: 2g, Fat: 7g, Fiber: 0.5g, Cholesterol: 0 mg, Sodium: 1012 mg, Potassium: 170 mg

Directions:

1. Begin by heating the broth in your fondue pot on the stove over medium heat. Stir in the Szechuan peppercorns, star anise, cinnamon stick, chili bean sauce, soy sauce, sesame oil, ginger, garlic, and green onions, bringing everything to a gentle simmer.
2. Add the sugar, Chinese cooking wine, and ground white pepper to the pot, stirring until the sugar dissolves and the spices are well integrated.
3. Let the mixture simmer for about 20-25 minutes to allow the flavors to meld together and the broth to become fragrant.
4. Once the Szechuan spicy broth has simmered, strain out the whole spices, such as the Szechuan peppercorns, star anise, ginger, and cinnamon stick, leaving a clear broth behind.
5. Carefully transfer the fondue pot to its base and set it up for serving. Adjust the fondue burner to ensure the broth stays hot, but not boiling, for dipping.
6. Serve the Szechuan spicy broth fondue with your choice of fresh vegetables, thinly sliced meats, and tofu. Have guests spear their chosen items with fondue forks and cook them in the hot broth until done to their liking.

Ethiopian Berbere Broth Fondue

 4 SERVINGS 15 MINUTES 30 MINUTES

Dive into the rich flavors of Ethiopia with this Berbere broth fondue, a spicy and aromatic experience that's perfect for dipping vegetables, meats, and bread. This fondue brings together the traditional spice of Berbere with a hearty broth base, creating a unique and memorable meal.

Equipment: Fondue pot, Cutting board, Kitchen knife

Ingredients:

- 6 cups Beef or Chicken Stock
- 2 tbsp Berbere Spice Mix
- 1 tbsp Olive Oil
- 2 Garlic Cloves, minced
- 1 Medium Onion, finely chopped
- 1 tsp Fresh Ginger, grated
- 1 Small Hot Chili Pepper, finely chopped (optional for extra heat)
- Salt to taste

Nutritional Information: Calories: 120, Protein: 8g, Carbohydrates: 6g, Fat: 7g, Fiber: 2g, Cholesterol: 10 mg, Sodium: 600 mg, Potassium: 300 mg

Directions:

1. Heat the olive oil in a saucepan over medium heat. Add the chopped onion, minced garlic, grated ginger, and chopped chili pepper (if using). Sauté until the onion is translucent and aromatic, about 5 minutes.
2. Stir in the Berbere spice mix and cook for another 2 minutes, making sure the spices are well-incorporated and fragrant.
3. Stirring to mix all the ingredients, slowly pour the beef or chicken stock into the pot. Simmer the mixture for a while.
4. As needed, add salt after tasting. To allow the flavors to mingle, boil the soup slowly for around 20 minutes.
5. Gently pour the broth into the fondue pot and place it on top of the burner. To keep the mixture simmering gently, adjust the heat.
6. Begin the fondue experience by dipping your choice of dippable items like cubed meats, vegetables, or chunks of crusty bread.

Greek Lemon & Oregano Broth Fondue

 6 SERVINGS 15 MINUTES 30 MINUTES

Experience the warmth and comfort of Greek cuisine with this aromatic lemon and oregano-infused broth, perfect for a Mediterranean-themed fondue night. The refreshing tang of lemon and the earthiness of oregano come together to create a broth fondue that will transport your taste buds to the sun-drenched coasts of Greece.

Equipment: Fondue pot, Stove or portable burner, Fondue forks

Ingredients:

- 6 cups Chicken or Vegetable Stock
- Zest of 2 Lemons
- 1/4 cup Fresh Lemon Juice
- 2 tbsp Olive Oil
- 4 Garlic Cloves, minced
- 2 tsp Dried Oregano
- 1 tsp Fresh Thyme Leaves
- 1 Bay Leaf
- To taste, add salt and freshly ground black pepper.
- Assorted Dippers: Cubed Feta Cheese, Pita Bread Pieces, Cherry Tomatoes, Sliced Bell Peppers, Cooked Chicken or Shrimp (optional), Sliced Zucchini

Nutritional Information: Calories: 120, Protein: 8g, Carbohydrates: 4g, Fat: 7g, Fiber: 0g, Cholesterol: 5mg, Sodium: 800mg, Potassium: 200mg"

Directions:

1. In a large pot over medium heat, combine the stock, lemon zest, lemon juice, olive oil, minced garlic, dried oregano, thyme leaves, and bay leaf, stirring to mingle the flavors.
2. The broth should be brought to a slow simmer before being covered and the heat turned down. Allow the broth to infuse for about 20 minutes, stirring occasionally.
3. Season the broth with salt and freshly ground black pepper to taste.
4. Carefully pour the seasoned broth into the fondue pot that's been set up with your heat source.
5. Arrange your chosen dippers on a platter and set up the fondue forks.
6. Encourage guests to spear their preferred dippers and submerge them into the hot, fragrant broth, cooking them until heated through and infused with flavor.
7. Add some optional cooked chicken or shrimp for a more robust option, ensuring they are reheated thoroughly in the hot broth.

Japanese Miso Broth Fondue

 6 SERVINGS 15 MINUTES 30 MINUTES

Discover the umami-rich flavors of Japan with this Japanese Miso Broth Fondue, a delightful and hearty broth that incorporates traditional miso paste and fragrant ingredients to create a warm and inviting dipping experience perfect for a variety of dippables, from fresh vegetables to thinly sliced meats.

Equipment: Fondue Pot, Stove, Ladle

Ingredients:

- 4 cups Dashi broth (you can either make your own with kombu seaweed and bonito flakes or use instant dashi)
- 3 tbsp Miso paste (either red, white, or a combination depending on desired flavor)
- 1 cup Water (to dilute miso paste)
- 2 tbsp Mirin (Japanese rice wine)
- 1 tbsp Soy sauce
- 1 tsp Ginger, freshly grated
- 1 Garlic clove, minced
- Assorted dippables (thinly sliced chicken, beef, tofu, mushrooms, and vegetables)

Nutritional Information: Calories: 45, Protein: 2g, Carbohydrates: 6g, Fat: 1g, Fiber: 1g, Cholesterol: 0 mg, Sodium: 900 mg, Potassium: 35 mg

Directions:

1. Start by preparing the dashi broth if you are making it from scratch. If using instant, follow the package instructions to dissolve the granules in 4 cups of boiling water.
2. In a separate bowl, thin out the miso paste with 1 cup of water to ensure it mixes smoothly into the broth and prevent lumps.
3. Heat the dashi broth in the pot on the stove over medium heat. Once it is hot, but not boiling, whisk in the miso mixture gently until fully integrated into the broth.
4. Stir in the mirin, soy sauce, ginger, and minced garlic. To allow the flavors to meld, bring the broth to a simmer and cook for five minutes.
5. Carefully transfer the broth into the fondue pot, set over its flame. Maintain low heat to keep the fondue at a slow simmer – you don't want it to boil, as this could compromise the delicate taste of the miso.
6. Arrange your selected dippables on plates around the fondue pot, and provide guests with fondue forks or skewers for dipping.
7. Have guests dip their chosen items into the hot miso broth until cooked to their preference and enjoy.

Spanish Chorizo & Paprika Broth Fondue

 6 SERVINGS 20 MINUTES 30 MINUTES

Dive into the bold flavors of Spain with this smoky Spanish Chorizo & Paprika Broth Fondue. It combines the spicy kick of chorizo, sweet paprika, and a garlic-infused broth to create an aromatic base perfect for dipping your favorite meats and vegetables. A twist on traditional fondue, this broth delight is sure to heat up your fondue pot and your night!

Equipment: Fondue pot, Cutting board, Sharp knife, Measuring cups and spoons

Ingredients:

- 1 tbsp Olive oil
- 4 cups Beef broth
- 1/2 cup Dry white wine
- 1 lb. Spanish chorizo, thinly sliced
- 1 Medium onion, finely chopped
- 3 Garlic cloves, minced
- 2 tsp Sweet paprika
- 1 tsp Smoked paprika
- 1/2 tsp Cayenne pepper (optional, for a spicy kick)
- 1 Bay leaf
- Salt and pepper to taste

Nutritional Information: Calories: 290, Protein: 13g, Carbohydrates: 6g, Fat: 22g, Fiber: 0.5g, Cholesterol: 45 mg, Sodium: 1350 mg, Potassium: 300 mg

Directions:

1. Heat the olive oil in a saucepan over a medium heat source. About 5 to 7 minutes after adding the chorizo pieces, heat them until they start to release their oils and become somewhat crispy.
2. Remove the chorizo with a slotted spoon and set aside. In the same saucepan, add the finely chopped onion and sauté until transparent.
3. Add the minced garlic, sweet paprika, smoked paprika, cayenne pepper (if using), and bay leaf to the onions, and sauté for another minute until fragrant.
4. After adding the white wine and beef broth, boil the mixture. Season with salt and pepper to taste.
5. Transfer the broth mixture to your fondue pot and keep it at a low simmer. You can add the chorizo slices back to the broth or serve them on the side for dipping.
6. Spear your chosen vegetables, meats, or seafood with fondue forks and submerge them into the hot broth until cooked to your desired level of doneness.

Middle Eastern Sumac Broth Fondue

 6 SERVINGS 21 MINUTES 30 MINUTES

Dive into a Middle Eastern-inspired fondue experience with this sumac broth fondue. Combining the tangy, lemony flavor of sumac with aromatic spices, this broth is perfect for dipping your favorite meats, vegetables, or bread. It's a unique twist on traditional fondue that will transport you to the spice-scented markets of the Middle East.

Equipment: Fondue pot, Stove, Skewers or fondue forks

Ingredients:

- 6 cups beef or chicken broth
- 2 tbsp ground sumac
- 1 medium onion, finely chopped
- 3 garlic cloves, minced
- 1 tsp ground cumin
- 1 tsp ground coriander
- 1/2 tsp ground cinnamon
- 1/2 tsp ground allspice
- 1/4 tsp cayenne pepper (adjust to taste)
- To taste, add salt and freshly ground black pepper.
- 1 tbsp olive oil
- Fresh cilantro or parsley for garnish, chopped

Nutritional Information: Calories: 80, Protein: 4g, Carbohydrates: 8g, Fat: 4g, Fiber: 1g, Cholesterol: 0mg, Sodium: 800mg, Potassium: 170mg

Directions:

1. In a medium saucepan, heat the olive oil over medium heat. Add the chopped onion and sauté until soft and translucent, about 5 minutes.
2. Stirring continually to keep it from burning, add the minced garlic to the pan and simmer for an additional minute.
3. Sprinkle in the ground sumac, cumin, coriander, cinnamon, allspice, and cayenne pepper. Cook for a couple of minutes until the spices become fragrant.
4. After adding the broth, slowly boil the mixture. Allow the flavors to mingle by cooking for around ten minutes.
5. If necessary, add more salt and black pepper after tasting the soup.
6. Carefully transfer the broth to your fondue pot, which should be set over a gentle flame to keep the broth hot for dipping.
7. Garnish the broth with chopped cilantro or parsley just before serving.
8. Serve with an array of dipping ingredients such as cubed beef, chicken, mushrooms, small potatoes, or crusty bread.

Korean Gochujang Broth Fondue

 4 SERVINGS 20 MINUTES 30 MINUTES

Indulge in a fiery Korean twist to your fondue night with this rich, spicy, and flavorful broth. Korean Gochujang Broth Fondue marries the robust taste of gochujang (Korean chili paste) with aromatic spices and vegetables, offering a bold and savory dipping experience that will thrill your taste buds and heat up your evening.

Equipment: Fondue Pot, Ladle, Chopsticks or Fondue Forks

Ingredients:

- 4 cups Beef or Chicken Stock
- 3 tbsp Gochujang (Korean chili paste)
- 1 tbsp Soy Sauce
- 1 tsp Sesame Oil
- 2 Garlic Cloves, minced
- 1-inch piece Ginger, grated
- 1/2 Medium Onion, thinly sliced
- 1 Green Onion, chopped
- 1/2 tsp Sugar
- 1/4 tsp Freshly Ground Black Pepper
- Assorted vegetables (such as mushrooms, bell peppers, and zucchini), sliced for dipping
- Assorted proteins (such as thinly sliced beef, chicken, tofu, or shrimp), prepared for dipping

Nutritional Information: Calories: 70, Protein: 3g, Carbohydrates: 10g, Fat: 2g, Fiber: 1g, Cholesterol: 0 mg, Sodium: 800 mg, Potassium: 200 mg

Directions:

1. In a large bowl, whisk together the gochujang, soy sauce, sesame oil, minced garlic, grated ginger, sugar, and black pepper until well combined.
2. Pour the beef or chicken stock into the fondue pot and set it over medium heat. Bring it to a gentle simmer.
3. Stir in the gochujang mixture into the simmering broth until fully incorporated.
4. Add the sliced onions to the broth, allowing them to soften and infuse their flavor for about 5 minutes.
5. Reduce the heat to low, where the broth maintains a gentle simmer but does not boil vigorously. This will be the temperature for dipping and cooking.
6. Arrange the sliced vegetables and proteins on separate plates around the fondue pot.
7. Skewer pieces of vegetables or proteins with fondue forks or chopsticks, and dip and swirl them in the hot broth until cooked to desired doneness. Typically, thinly sliced meats will cook in about 30 seconds to a minute, while vegetables will take a bit longer, depending on their thickness and density.

Cajun Creole Broth Fondue

 4 SERVINGS   20 MINUTES   30 MINUTES

Savor the bold flavors of the Bayou with this spicy Cajun Creole Broth Fondue. Perfect for those who love their fondue with a kick, it's ideal for cooking seafood, chicken, or vegetables while enjoying a unique communal dining experience. A fusion of Cajun seasonings and a savory broth creates the perfect dip for an unforgettable taste adventure.

Equipment: Fondue pot, Burner, Ladle

Ingredients:

- 4 cups Beef or Chicken Broth
- 1/2 cup Onions, finely chopped
- 1/2 cup Celery, finely chopped
- 1/2 cup Green Bell Pepper, finely chopped
- 3 cloves Garlic, minced
- 14.5 oz can Diced Tomatoes (with juices)
- 2 tbsp Cajun Seasoning
- 1 tsp Dried Thyme
- 1 tsp Dried Oregano
- 2 Bay Leaves
- 1/2 tsp Cayenne Pepper (adjust to taste)
- Salt and Black Pepper to taste
- 1 tbsp Worcestershire Sauce
- 1 tbsp Hot Sauce (optional for extra heat)
- Fresh Parsley, chopped for garnish

Directions:

1. In the fondue pot, combine the beef or chicken broth, onions, celery, green bell pepper, and garlic. Stir the liquid over medium heat until it starts to simmer.
2. Stir in the canned diced tomatoes with their juices, Cajun seasoning, dried thyme, dried oregano, bay leaves, cayenne pepper, salt, and black pepper.
3. After bringing the broth to a mild boil, lower the heat so that it simmers. To allow the flavors to mingle, cook for ten minutes.
4. Stir in the spicy sauce (if using) and Worcestershire sauce. If needed, adjust the seasoning by tasting it.
5. Reduce the burner flame to low, ensuring the fondue remains warm but not boiling. Skewer your choice of dippables and cook in the simmering broth until done to your liking.
6. Garnish with fresh parsley before serving.
7. To maintain the heat throughout the dining experience, adjust the burner as needed.

Nutritional Information: Calories: 70, Protein: 5g, Carbohydrates: 8g, Fat: 1g, Fiber: 1g, Cholesterol: 5 mg, Sodium: 750 mg, Potassium: 320 mg

Jamaican Jerk Broth Fondue

 4 SERVINGS   20 MINUTES   30 MINUTES

This Jamaican Jerk Broth Fondue brings the vibrant tastes of the Caribbean to your table with its spicy, flavorful broth. Perfect for dipping meats and vegetables, it promises a mouthwatering experience with every bite and a delightful way to spice up your fondue night.

Equipment: Fondue pot, Stove, Chopping board, Knife

Ingredients:

- 4 cups Chicken broth
- 1 small Onion, finely diced
- 3 cloves Garlic, minced
- 2 tbsp Jamaican jerk seasoning
- 1 tsp Thyme, dried
- 1 Scotch bonnet pepper, finely chopped (optional for extra heat)
- 1 tsp Ginger, freshly grated
- 2 tbsp Soy sauce
- 1 tbsp Brown sugar
- 1 tbsp Lime juice
- Freshly ground black pepper, to taste
- Assortment of fondue dippers (cubed chicken, beef, shrimp, bell peppers, mushrooms, etc.)

Directions:

1. In a large saucepan over medium heat, combine chicken broth, diced onion, minced garlic, Jamaican jerk seasoning, dried thyme, Scotch bonnet pepper (if using), and grated ginger. Bring the mixture to a simmer.
2. Lower the heat to a low level and thoroughly mix in the soy sauce, brown sugar, and lime juice. To let the flavors mingle, simmer for around 15 minutes, stirring from time to time.
3. After tasting the soup, taste again and add more salt and freshly ground black pepper if needed.
4. Gently pour the heated broth into your fondue pot and place it over a low heat to maintain its warmth.
5. Arrange your chosen fondue dippers on a platter. Skewer your choice of dipper and submerge it in the hot Jamaican Jerk Broth Fondue, cooking until done to your liking. Be cautious with the Scotch Bonnet as it brings a significant amount of heat.
6. Enjoy your exotic fondue experience by dipping, swirling, and savoring each flavorful bite.

Nutritional Information: Calories: 70, Protein: 5g, Carbohydrates: 10g, Fat: 1g, Fiber: 1g, Cholesterol: 0 mg, Sodium: 940 mg, Potassium: 200 mg

Russian Dill & Mustard Broth Fondue

 6 SERVINGS 15 MINUTES 30 MINUTES

Embark on a culinary journey to the heart of Russia with this aromatic and hearty Dill & Mustard Broth Fondue. The bold mustard flavors meld perfectly with the fresh dill, creating a broth that is both invigorating and comforting, perfect for dipping your favorite meats and vegetables.

Equipment: Fondue pot, Cutting board, Sharp knife

Ingredients:

- 6 cups Beef broth
- 1/4 cup Fresh dill, chopped
- 1/4 cup Dijon mustard
- 2 tbsp Whole grain mustard
- 1/4 cup Dry white wine
- 1 tsp Worcestershire sauce
- 1 Garlic clove, minced
- 1/2 tsp Black pepper, freshly ground
- 1/2 lb Thinly sliced beef tenderloin (as a dipping ingredient)
- 1/2 lb Fresh shrimp, peeled and deveined (as a dipping ingredient)
- Assorted vegetables (such as bell peppers, mushrooms, and cherry tomatoes) for dipping

Nutritional Information: Calories: 60, Protein: 4g, Carbohydrates: 4g, Fat: 2g, Fiber: 1g, Cholesterol: 5 mg, Sodium: 800 mg, Potassium: 100 mg

Directions:

1. In the fondue pot, combine beef broth, chopped fresh dill, Dijon mustard, whole grain mustard, dry white wine, Worcestershire sauce, minced garlic, and freshly ground black pepper.
2. To make sure all the ingredients are well incorporated, place the fondue pot over medium heat and bring the sauce to a simmer, stirring from time to time.
3. Once the broth is simmering, reduce the heat to low and allow it to gently simmer for 15 minutes for the flavors to meld together.
4. Meanwhile, prepare the dipping ingredients: thinly slice the beef tenderloin, and ensure the shrimp is peeled and deveined; cut the vegetables into bite-sized pieces.
5. Arrange the raw meats and vegetables on a serving platter around the fondue pot.
6. Once the broth is ready, guests can spear their chosen dipping ingredients with fondue forks and cook them in the hot broth until done to their liking.
7. To balance the flavors of the broth and dipped foods, serve individual plates with dipping sauces (try horseradish cream or a chilled yogurt sauce).

Turkish Delight Broth Fondue

 6 SERVINGS 25 MINUTES 30 MINUTES

Immerse yourself in the exotic flavors of the East with this aromatic Turkish Delight Broth Fondue. Inspired by the classic sweet treat, this fondue combines the essence of rose, the depth of spices, and the purity of a delicate broth, offering you a unique dipping experience for your favorite meats and vegetables.

Equipment: Fondue pot, heat source (burner or candle), skewers or fondue forks

Ingredients:

- 6 cups beef or vegetable broth
- 1 cup strong-brewed Turkish coffee
- 1 tablespoon rose water
- 1 teaspoon ground cardamom
- 1 cinnamon stick
- 3 cloves
- 1/2 teaspoon black pepper, freshly ground
- 1/4 teaspoon ground nutmeg
- Pinch of saffron (optional, for a luxurious touch)
- Assorted dipping ingredients (such as beef, lamb, chicken, mushrooms, bell peppers, and zucchini), pre-cooked if necessary and cut into bite-sized pieces

Nutritional Information: Calories: 98, Protein: 6g, Carbohydrates: 4g, Fat: 6g, Fiber: 0.5g, Cholesterol: 0 mg, Sodium: 897 mg, Potassium: 170 mg

Directions:

1. In a medium saucepan, combine the beef or vegetable broth and the brewed Turkish coffee. Over medium heat, bring the mixture to a moderate simmer.
2. Stir in the rose water, ground cardamom, cinnamon stick, cloves, black pepper, ground nutmeg, and saffron if using. Reduce the heat to low and let the broth infuse with the spices for about 10 minutes, occasionally stirring.
3. Carefully pour the spiced broth into the fondue pot, set over your chosen heat source. Adjust the temperature so the broth maintains a gentle simmer – not a full boil.
4. Skewer your desired dipping ingredients with fondue forks and submerge into the Turkish Delight broth, cooking until done to your liking. Typically, meats will take 3-5 minutes to cook through, while vegetables will be ready in 1-2 minutes, depending on size and type.
5. Serve immediately, ensuring each guest has a fondue fork or skewer for dipping.

Oil Fondue Indulgences

Crispy Golden Tempura Fondue

 4 SERVINGS   25 MINUTES   20 MINUTES

Indulge in a blend of East meets West with this Crispy Golden Tempura Fondue. A delightful twist to your fondue experience, it is perfect for those who love to dip their sweet and savory bites into hot oil for a quick, golden cook. Enjoy this interactive and delicious way to entertain guests or treat your family to a fun meal that crackles with excitement.

Equipment: Fondue Pot, Thermometer, Chopsticks or Fondue Forks

Ingredients:

- 2 cups Vegetable Oil, for frying
- 1 cup All-Purpose Flour
- 1 Egg, cold
- 1 cup Ice-cold Water
- 1/2 cup Cornstarch
- 1 tsp Baking Soda
- Various raw dipping ingredients (such as shrimp, vegetables like bell pepper slices, mushrooms, broccoli florets, and slices of your favorite fruits like apples or bananas for a sweet option)
- Salt, to taste

Nutritional Information: Calories: 215, Protein: 4g, Carbohydrates: 27g, Fat: 10g, Fiber: 1g, Cholesterol: 41 mg, Sodium: 300 mg, Potassium: 88 mg

Directions:

1. Heat the vegetable oil in your fondue pot to 375 degrees F (190 degrees C). Use the thermometer to ensure accurate temperature.
2. In a separate bowl, lightly beat the cold egg, then mix in the ice-cold water.
3. In another bowl, combine the all-purpose flour, cornstarch, and baking soda. Gently mix the dry ingredients to ensure they are well blended.
4. Slowly pour the egg and water mixture into the bowl with the dry ingredients. Stir gently, being careful not to overmix; the batter should be lumpy.
5. Pat your dipping ingredients dry to prevent splattering. Then, one by one, dip them into the batter to coat evenly.
6. Using chopsticks or fondue forks, carefully lower the battered ingredients into the hot oil. Cook for two to four minutes, depending on the contents, or until the batter is crispy and golden.
7. Once the food is cooked, take it out and place it on a platter covered with paper towels to absorb any remaining oil.. Sprinkle with a little salt while they're still warm.
8. Continue this process, cooking small batches to maintain the oil temperature and ensure each piece gets evenly cooked.
9. Serve right away to enjoy the delicate tempura taste straight or with your preferred dipping sauces.

Bourbon BBQ Meatball Fondue

 6 SERVINGS   25 MINUTES   15 MINUTES

Indulge in a delectable twist to traditional fondue with our Bourbon BBQ Meatball Fondue. This hearty and flavorful dish blends the richness of bourbon with the sweetness of barbecue, creating a savory dipping sauce that complements perfectly seasoned meatballs fried to perfection. Dive into an interactive dining experience that's ideal for gatherings and guaranteed to leave your guests raving.

Equipment: Fondue pot, Skewers, Mixing bowl

Ingredients:

- 1 lb Ground beef
- 1/4 cup Breadcrumbs
- 1 Egg
- 1/4 cup Finely chopped onion
- Salt and pepper, to taste
- 1 cup Bourbon whiskey
- 1 cup Barbecue sauce
- 2 cups Vegetable oil
- 1/4 cup Honey
- 1 tbsp Worcestershire sauce
- 1 Garlic clove, minced
- Fresh parsley, chopped (for garnish)

Nutritional Information: Calories: 490, Protein: 22g, Carbohydrates: 30g, Fat: 29g, Fiber: 1g, Cholesterol: 80 mg, Sodium: 850 mg, Potassium: 360 mg

Directions:

1. Ground beef, breadcrumbs, egg, finely chopped onion, salt, and pepper should all be combined in a mixing dish. Mix until all ingredients are well amalgamated.
2. Shape the mixture into 1-inch meatballs, and set them aside.
3. In your fondue pot, heat vegetable oil to 375°F (190°C) – ideally, you should use a thermometer to ensure the correct temperature.
4. Once the oil is heated, fry meatballs in batches until they're evenly browned and cooked through, which should take about 4 to 5 minutes. Make sure not to overcrowd the pot.
5. As the meatballs are cooking, prepare your bourbon BBQ sauce. Combine the bourbon, honey, barbecue sauce, Worcestershire sauce, and minced garlic in a separate skillet over medium heat. For ten minutes, bring to a gentle simmer so that the flavors may mingle and the alcohol can evaporate.
6. When the meatballs are done, move them to a platter lined with paper towels so that any extra oil may be drained off.
7. Serve the freshly fried meatballs alongside your warm bourbon BBQ sauce. Provide skewers for your guests to dip the meatballs into the sauce.
8. Garnish with chopped parsley for an added touch of flavor and color.

Crunchy Coconut Shrimp Fondue

 4 SERVINGS   20 MINUTES   10 MINUTES

Dive into tropical flavors with this Crunchy Coconut Shrimp Fondue, where succulent shrimp are coated in a crisp coconut breadcrumb mix and then submerged into hot oil until perfectly golden. It's an indulgent way to enjoy seafood with a fondue twist, perfect for sharing at your next gathering.

Equipment: Fondue pot, Skewer sticks, Paper towels, Deep-frying thermometer, Bowls

Ingredients:

- 1 lb Large shrimp, peeled and deveined
- 1 cup Sweetened shredded coconut
- 1 cup Panko breadcrumbs
- 2 Large eggs
- 1/2 cup All-purpose flour
- Salt, to taste
- Pepper, to taste
- Vegetable oil for frying
- For the dip: 1/2 cup Orange marmalade; 1/4 cup Dijon mustard; 1 tablespoon Honey; 1 tablespoon Lime juice

Nutritional Information: Calories: 450, Protein: 24g, Carbohydrates: 45g, Fat: 20g, Fiber: 3g, Cholesterol: 178 mg, Sodium: 1200 mg, Potassium: 230 mg

Directions:

1. Begin by setting up your fondue pot filled with vegetable oil on a stable surface. Using a deep-frying thermometer to keep an eye on the temperature, heat the oil to 375°F.
2. As the oil heats up, get the shrimp ready. Put the flour in a shallow basin and season with salt and pepper. Beat the eggs in a second bowl. In a third bowl, combine shredded coconut and Panko breadcrumbs.
3. Pat the shrimp dry with paper towels. First, coat each shrimp completely with the coconut breadcrumb mixture, shake off any excess flour, and then dip it into the beaten eggs.
4. Once the oil has reached the desired temperature, use the fondue skewers to carefully lower the coated shrimp into the hot oil. Work in batches to avoid overcrowding, frying the shrimp until they are golden brown and crispy, usually 2-3 minutes per side.
5. Remove the shrimp with a slotted spoon and place them on a platter covered with paper towels to drain any excess oil.
6. In a bowl, thoroughly mix orange marmalade, Dijon mustard, honey, and lime juice to make the dip.
7. Serve the hot crunchy shrimp with the marmalade dip and encourage guests to spear shrimp with fondue forks and dip into the sauce.

Garlic Herb Steak Bites Fondue

 4 SERVINGS   20 MINUTES   10 MINUTES

Savor the robust flavors of tender steak bites seasoned with a harmonious blend of garlic and herbs, cooked to perfection in a sizzling oil fondue. This indulgent recipe offers a delightful way to enjoy steak in bite-sized pieces, perfect for a social dining experience that's both interactive and delectable.

Equipment: Fondue pot, Fondue forks or skewers, Cutting board, Chef's knife

Ingredients:

- One-pound sirloin steak, diced into one-inch pieces
- 2 tbsp fresh parsley, finely chopped
- 1 tbsp fresh rosemary, minced
- 2 garlic cloves, minced
- 1/2 tsp sea salt
- freshly ground 1/4 tsp black pepper
- two cups oil for frying (such as peanut or safflower oil)

Nutritional Information: Calories: 498, Protein: 25g, Carbohydrates: 1g, Fat: 44g, Fiber: 0.2g, Cholesterol: 69 mg, Sodium: 319 mg, Potassium: 372 mg

Directions:

1. Pat the steak bites dry with paper towels to ensure proper browning during the fondue process.
2. To make the herb mix, combine the minced garlic, minced rosemary, minced parsley, sea salt, and black pepper in a small bowl.
3. Place the steak bites in a large mixing bowl and sprinkle them with the herb blend, tossing until the cubes are evenly coated.
4. Fill your fondue pot about 1/2 full with the oil and heat to around 375°F. To make sure the oil is the right temperature for cooking the steak bites, use a cooking thermometer.
5. Once the oil is heated, skewer the herbed steak bites with the fondue forks.
6. The skewered steak bites should be cooked for a minimum of one to two minutes, depending on the desired doneness. Usually, this means one minute for rare, 1.5 minutes for medium-rare, and two minutes for well-done.
7. After taking the cooked steak bits out of the oil, give them a little rest on a fresh plate covered with paper towels so that any extra oil may be drained out.
8. Serve hot and enjoy with your favorite fondue dipping sauces, such as a creamy horseradish sauce, a tangy béarnaise, or a bold chimichurri.

Cajun Catfish Fry Fondue

 4 SERVINGS 20 MINUTES 15 MINUTES

Delve into the spicy flavors of the South with this Cajun Catfish Fry Fondue. Serve hot and perfectly seasoned with a blend of Cajun spices, this meal takes the traditional fondue experience to a new social level. Enjoy crispy, golden-brown catfish pieces that have been fried to perfection and are ready for dipping and sharing amongst friends.

Equipment: Fondue pot, Fryer or deep saucepan, Tongs

Ingredients:

- 1 lb Catfish fillets, cut into fondue-sized pieces
- Two cups of vegetable or peanut oil for frying
- 1 cup Buttermilk
- 1 cup Cornmeal
- 1 Tbsp Cajun seasoning
- 1 tsp Garlic powder
- 1 tsp Onion powder
- ½ tsp Cayenne pepper (adjust according to spice preference)
- ½ tsp Dried thyme
- ½ tsp Salt
- ¼ tsp Ground black pepper
- Lemon wedges and parsley for garnish

Nutritional Information: Calories: 298, Protein: 23g, Carbohydrates: 15g, Fat: 14g, Fiber: 1g, Cholesterol: 58 mg, Sodium: 597 mg, Potassium: 562 mg

Directions:

1. Begin by heating the oil in a fryer or deep saucepan to 375°F (190°C). You'll want to maintain this temperature for optimal frying conditions once you start cooking the catfish.
2. Transfer the buttermilk to a shallow basin and let it warm up. In another shallow bowl, mix together cornmeal, Cajun seasoning, garlic powder, onion powder, cayenne pepper, thyme, salt, and black pepper to create your dredging mixture.
3. Dip each piece of catfish first into the buttermilk, ensuring it's fully coated, and then dredge in the cornmeal mixture until it's completely covered with the spicy blend.
4. Once the oil has reached the right temperature, carefully place the coated catfish pieces into the hot oil using tongs. To prevent uneven cooking due to crowding, fry the fish in batches. Fry for 5 to 7 minutes or until they turn a delightful golden brown and float to the surface, indicating they're done.
5. When the catfish are carefully removed from the oil with tongs, place them on a dish covered with paper towels so that any leftover oil may be absorbed.
6. Once all of the catfish has been fried, place it on a serving dish, top with some chopped parsley and lemon wedges, and serve right away with your preferred dipping sauces and a variety of vibrant veggies for a hearty fondue feast.

Asian Sesame Beef Fondue

 4 SERVINGS 15 MINUTES 20 MINUTES

Delve into the delectable flavors of the East with this Asian Sesame Beef Fondue. Perfect for an interactive dining experience, this recipe combines tender beef with the aromatic hints of sesame and soy sauce, ensuring each bite is a delightful savor. Gather around the fondue pot and let the magic of Asian spices tantalize your taste buds.

Equipment: Fondue pot, Fondue forks or skewers, Stove, Medium bowl

Ingredients:

- One pound of tender beef, sliced into 1-inch pieces
- Two cups of canola or peanut oil for frying
- 3 tbsp soy sauce
- 2 tbsp brown sugar
- 1 tbsp toasted sesame oil
- 2 tsp fresh ginger, finely grated
- 2 garlic cloves, minced
- Red pepper flakes, 1/2 tsp (optional for extra heat) 2 green onions, thinly sliced for garnish
- Toasted sesame seeds, for garnish
- Marinade Ingredients: 2 tbsp soy sauce; 1 tbsp rice vinegar; 1 1/2 tsp toasted sesame oil; 1 tsp brown sugar; 1 garlic clove, minced; 1/2 tsp fresh ginger, grated

Nutritional Information: Calories: 560, Protein: 24g, Carbohydrates: 5g, Fat: 50g, Fiber: 0g, Cholesterol: 68 mg, Sodium: 570 mg, Potassium: 360 mg

Directions:

1. In a medium bowl, combine all of the marinade ingredients. Mixing the liquid thoroughly and dissolving the sugar requires whisking.
2. When the meat cubes are completely coated, add them to the marinade and toss again. For a more flavorful marinade, leave the beef in the bowl covered and refrigerated for up to 24 hours.
3. When ready to cook, fill the fondue pot with the peanut or canola oil and heat it on the stove until the oil reaches 375°F. Be sure to follow your fondue pot's instructions for oil fondue to ensure safety.
4. While the oil is heating, mix the soy sauce, brown sugar, toasted sesame oil, ginger, garlic, and red pepper flakes in a small bowl to create the dipping sauce.
5. Carefully transfer the heated oil to the fondue pot stand and maintain it at a safe cooking temperature, usually by adjusting the burner beneath.
6. Pat the marinated beef cubes dry with paper towels to prevent splattering.
7. Skewer the beef cubes with fondue forks and carefully lower them into the hot oil. Cook each piece of beef until it reaches the desired doneness, typically about 2-3 minutes for medium-rare.
8. After the steak is done, take it out of the pan and let any excess drip off before dipping it into the sesame-soy sauce concoction.
9. Garnish the beef with sliced green onions and toasted sesame seeds.
10. Continue cooking and enjoying the beef with guests, encouraging them to try different cooking times to find their perfect level of doneness.

Savory Sausage & Pepper Fondue

 6 SERVINGS 15 MINUTES 15 MINUTES

Savor the union of smoky sausages and sweet bell peppers in this unique and hearty oil fondue indulgence. Perfect for sharing around the table, this recipe is a meat lover's twist on a classic fondue that offers a robust flavor profile and a fun, interactive dining experience.

Equipment: Fondue pot, Metal fondue forks, Cutting board, Knife

Ingredients:

- 1 lb Your favorite sausages, cut into bite-sized pieces
- One quart of peanut or vegetable oil for frying
- One red bell pepper, chopped into small bits
- One green bell pepper, sliced into small pieces
- 1 Yellow bell pepper, cut into bite-sized pieces
- 2 tsp Garlic powder
- 2 tsp Smoked paprika
- Salt and pepper, to taste
- Assorted dipping sauces (optional)

Nutritional Information: Calories: 350, Protein: 16g, Carbohydrates: 5g, Fat: 30g (varies with oil absorption), Fiber: 1g, Cholesterol: 40 mg, Sodium: 480 mg, Potassium: 230 mg

Directions:

1. Preheat your fondue pot to the manufacturer's instructions for oil fondue, typically around 350°F (175°C).
2. After adding the vegetable oil to the fondue pot, heat it to the proper temperature. Use a cooking thermometer to ensure accuracy.
3. In a large bowl, toss the bite-sized sausage pieces with garlic powder, smoked paprika, salt, and pepper until they're well-coated.
4. Using metal fondue forks, carefully skewer a piece of sausage and a piece of bell pepper together, ensuring they are secure.
5. Once the oil is hot, lower the skewered sausage and pepper into the oil and fry for about 2-3 minutes or until the sausage is golden brown and cooked through.
6. The cooked sausage and pepper should be taken out of the oil and placed on a plate covered with paper towels to absorb any remaining oil.
7. Repeat the process with the remaining sausage and pepper pieces. Ensure everyone cooks their skewers for a safe length of time.
8. Serve hot alongside your favorite dipping sauces such as spicy mustard, barbecue sauce, or garlic aioli.

Panko Crusted Mushroom Fondue

 4 SERVINGS 15 MINUTES 5 MINUTES

Dive into the savory experience of Panko Crusted Mushroom Fondue, where the umami of mushrooms meets the satisfying crunch of golden panko. A perfect symphony of texture and flavor, this dish is sure to be a crowd-pleaser at any gathering.

Equipment: Fondue Pot, Skewers, Stovetop, Deep Frying Thermometer

Ingredients:

- 16 oz (1 lb) Button mushrooms, stems removed, cleaned
- 1 cup Panko breadcrumbs
- 2 Large eggs, beaten
- 1/2 cup All-purpose flour
- 1 tsp Salt
- 1/2 tsp Black pepper
- 1 tsp Garlic powder
- Two cups of peanut or vegetable oil (for frying)
- Your favorite dipping sauces (e.g., garlic aioli, ranch, or teriyaki)

Nutritional Information: Calories: 312, Protein: 6g, Carbohydrates: 22g, Fat: 22g, Fiber: 1.5g, Cholesterol: 93 mg, Sodium: 452 mg, Potassium: 299 mg

Directions:

1. Prepare your fondue pot by filling it with the vegetable or peanut oil, making sure not to exceed the maximum fill line. Reposition the oil on its stand with a heat source underneath and heat it to 350°F/175°C on the cooktop.
2. As the oil heats, prepare a breading station by setting out three shallow dishes: one for flour, one for beaten eggs, and a third for mixing the panko breadcrumbs with the black pepper, salt, and garlic powder.
3. Shake off excess flour after lightly rolling each mushroom in the flour. Once it's well covered, dip it into the beaten eggs and then press it into the seasoned panko mixture.
4. Once all the mushrooms are breaded, begin frying them in batches to avoid overcrowding. Skewer each mushroom and dip it into the hot oil, frying it for about 2-3 minutes or until it's golden brown and crispy.
5. After taking out of the oil, set the mushrooms on a platter covered with paper towels to absorb any leftover oil. Top with your preferred dipping sauces and serve right away.

Zesty Lemon Chicken Fondue

 4 SERVINGS   15 MINUTES   10 MINUTES

Dive into this tantalizing Zesty Lemon Chicken Fondue, a citrus-infused delight that's perfect for brightening up your gatherings. With the tangy zestiness of lemon and the tender bite of chicken, it's a lively centerpiece for any fondue party that promises an invigorating taste adventure with every dip.

Equipment: Fondue Pot, Fondue Forks, Stove or Portable Burner, Meat Thermometer (optional)

Ingredients:

- One pound of boneless chicken breast, sliced into little pieces
- 2 cups Canola Oil, or enough for submerging chicken in fondue pot
- 1 Lemon, zest and juice
- 2 tbsp Honey
- 1 tsp Garlic Powder
- 1/2 tsp Paprika
- 1/2 tsp Dried Oregano
- Salt and Pepper, to taste
- Fresh Parsley, chopped for garnish
- Lemon Slices, for serving

Nutritional Information: Calories: 290, Protein: 25g, Carbohydrates: 7g, Fat: 18g, Fiber: 0.7g, Cholesterol: 65 mg, Sodium: 80 mg, Potassium: 370 mg

Directions:

1. Mix the dried oregano, paprika, lemon zest, lemon juice, honey, garlic powder, and a dash of salt and pepper in a bowl. In order to give the chicken cubes extra flavor, marinate them in the refrigerator for at least 30 minutes or up to two hours after tossing them thoroughly in the marinade.
2. When ready to cook, heat the canola oil in the fondue pot on the stove or portable burner until it reaches 350-375°F. To make sure the oil is the proper temperature for safe frying, use a meat thermometer.
3. Carefully place the marinated chicken cubes onto the fondue forks. Lower the cubes into the heated oil while working in batches, and fry for three to four minutes, or until the chicken is cooked through and golden brown. Ensure the cooked chicken reaches an internal temperature of 165°F.
4. After the chicken is done, take it out of the pan and put it on a platter covered with paper towels to drain any extra oil.
5. With fresh lemon slices and chopped parsley on top, serve the Zesty Lemon Chicken pieces right away.
6. These chicken bites can be accompanied by an array of sauces, such as aioli, herbed yogurt, or a tangy citrus dip for extra zest.

Spicy Buffalo Cauliflower Fondue

 4 SERVINGS   15 MINUTES   20 MINUTES

Experience the zesty kick of buffalo wings in vegetarian form with this Spicy Buffalo Cauliflower Fondue. It's an innovative twist on fondue that packs a punch with its bold flavors and offers a guilt-free indulgence for spice lovers and fondue enthusiasts alike. This dish is perfect for those looking to enjoy the communal fondue experience while keeping it light and plant-based.

Equipment: Fondue pot, Saucepan, Slotted spoon, Paper towels

Ingredients:

- 1 head Cauliflower, cut into bite-sized florets
- Two cups of frying oil (canola or vegetable)
- 1/2 cup Buffalo sauce
- 1/4 cup Unsalted butter
- 1 tsp Garlic powder
- 1 tsp Paprika
- 1/2 tsp Salt
- 1/4 tsp Black pepper
- 1/4 tsp Cayenne pepper (adjust for heat preference)
- Blue cheese or ranch dressing, for dipping
- Celery sticks, for serving

Nutritional Information: Calories: 207, Protein: 3g, Carbohydrates: 9g, Fat: 18g, Fiber: 3g, Cholesterol: 31 mg, Sodium: 1092 mg, Potassium: 431 mg

Directions:

1. Pour oil into your fondue pot to about halfway full and preheat to 375°F (190°C). This will help you fry food at a constant temperature.
2. While the oil is heating, prepare the buffalo sauce mixture. Combine the buffalo sauce, butter, paprika, garlic powder, black pepper, and cayenne pepper in a skillet over medium heat. Stir until the butter is melted and the ingredients are well combined. To keep the sauce warm, turn the heat down to low.
3. Cauliflower florets should be added gradually in batches while the oil is heated to prevent crowding. Fry for about 6-8 minutes, or until they are golden brown and crispy.
4. With a slotted spoon, take the cauliflower out of the oil and allow any extra to drain off. To absorb any extra oil, put the fried cauliflower on a platter covered with paper towels.
5. Make sure every piece of fried cauliflower is equally coated by tossing it in the prepared buffalo sauce mixture.
6. After moving the coated cauliflower to a platter, serve it right away with ranch or blue cheese dressing available for dipping. Serve with carrot sticks.

Classic Fondue Bourguignonne

 4 SERVINGS 20 MINUTES 10 MINUTES

Fondue Bourguignonne is a traditional French dish where guests cook their own pieces of meat in hot oil at the table. It's a lively and entertaining way to spend dinner with loved ones. This classic version brings a rich, savory experience perfect for those who appreciate the ceremony of cooking together.

Equipment: Fondue pot, Fondue forks or skewers, Heat source (sterno or electric fondue burner)

Ingredients:

- One quart of frying peanut or canola oil
- 1.5 lb Beef tenderloin, cut into ¾-inch cubes
- 1 tsp Salt
- ½ tsp Black pepper
- 2 tbsp Mixed herbs (such as thyme, rosemary, and oregano), finely chopped
- 1 Garlic clove, cut in half
- Assorted dipping sauces (such as béarnaise, horseradish cream, garlic aioli, or peppercorn sauce)

Nutritional Information: Calories: 540, Protein: 28g, Carbohydrates: 1g, Fat: 48g, Fiber: 0g, Cholesterol: 85 mg, Sodium: 635 mg, Potassium: 360 mg

Directions:

1. To add a hint of garlic to the oil, rub the cut edges of the garlic clove within the fondue pot. Discard the garlic afterward.
2. Fill the fondue pot no more than 1/2 full with vegetable oil (peanut or canola oil works best for its higher smoke point). Place the pot on the burner and heat the oil to 375°F. Always monitor the pot when the oil is heating.
3. While the oil is heating, season the cubes of beef tenderloin with salt, black pepper, and mixed herbs.
4. Once the oil has reached the desired temperature, each diner spears a piece of beef with a fondue fork and places it into the hot oil.
5. Cook the meat to each individual's preference: 30-45 seconds for rare, 45-60 seconds for medium-rare, or 60-90 seconds for well-done.
6. Serve the cooked beef with a variety of dipping sauces on the side for each person to enjoy.

Italian Mozzarella Stick Fondue

 6 SERVINGS 20 MINUTES 5 MINUTES

What could be more indulgent than golden, crispy mozzarella sticks dipped into a warm bath of savory oil fondue? The Italian Mozzarella Stick Fondue marries the comforting pull of melted cheese with the crisp exterior that only deep frying can offer. It's a perfect twist on traditional fondue that invites you to dip and savor in a shared, convivial experience. Mangiamo!

Equipment: Fondue pot, Deep Fryer or Heavy Bottomed Pan, Tongs, Paper Towels

Ingredients:

- 1 lb Mozzarella Cheese, cut into 3-inch by ½-inch sticks
- 2 cups All-Purpose Flour
- 4 Large Eggs, beaten
- 2 cups Italian Seasoned Breadcrumbs
- 1 teaspoon Garlic Powder
- 1 teaspoon Onion Powder
- ½ teaspoon Dried Oregano
- ½ teaspoon Dried Basil
- Salt and Pepper, to taste
- Vegetable Oil, for frying
- Marinara Sauce, for dipping

Nutritional Information: Calories: 430, Protein: 28g, Carbohydrates: 35g, Fat: 18g, Fiber: 2g, Cholesterol: 120mg, Sodium: 720mg, Potassium: 161mg

Directions:

1. Start by heating the vegetable oil in your fondue pot. The oil should be at 350°F to ensure the mozzarella sticks cook properly.
2. As the oil warms up, prepare a breading station featuring three small dishes: one containing flour, another containing beaten eggs, and a third containing a mixture of Italian seasoned breadcrumbs, onion powder, garlic powder, dried oregano, and dried basil. Season the breadcrumb mixture, as well as the flour, with salt and pepper to taste.
3. Coat each mozzarella stick in flour, gently tapping off any excess. Then, dip the stick into the beaten egg, ensuring all sides are coated. Finally, coat the stick well with the seasoned breadcrumb mixture.
4. Once the oil is at the correct temperature, use tongs to dip and fry the mozzarella sticks in batches, careful not to overcrowd the pot. Fry for approximately a minute, or until crispy and golden brown.
5. Using tongs, remove the sticks, and let them to drain on a dish covered with paper towels to absorb any remaining oil.
6. Serve the mozzarella sticks immediately with warm marinara sauce on the side for dipping.

Sweet and Sour Pork Fondue

 6 SERVINGS 20 MINUTES 10 MINUTES

Delight in the savory goodness of Sweet and Sour Pork Fondue, a perfect blend of succulent pork pieces dipped in a tangy sauce that tantalizes the taste buds. Ideal for interactive dining, this fondue brings a touch of Asian flair to your table. Gather your friends and family for a fun and delicious experience.

Equipment: Fondue pot, Fondue forks or skewers, Deep-fry thermometer

Ingredients:

- One pound of delicate pork, sliced into 1-inch pieces
- 2 cups Vegetable oil (for frying)
- Salt and pepper, to taste
- 1 cup All-purpose flour
- For the Sweet and Sour Sauce:
- 1/2 cup Sugar
- 1/4 cup White vinegar
- 1/4 cup Apple cider vinegar
- 3 Tbsp Soy sauce; 1/2 cup Ketchup
- 1 tsp Garlic, minced
- Mix 1 tablespoon cornstarch with 2 tablespoons water.
- Garnish:
- Sesame seeds (optional)
- Thinly sliced green onions (optional)

Nutritional Information: Calories: 400, Protein: 23g, Carbohydrates: 40g, Fat: 16g, Fiber: 0.5g, Cholesterol: 60 mg, Sodium: 600 mg, Potassium: 380 mg

Directions:

1. Begin by preparing the sweet and sour sauce. Combine the sugar, ketchup, apple cider vinegar, white vinegar, soy sauce, and garlic in a skillet over medium heat. Bring the mixture to a simmer.
2. After bringing the liquid to a simmer, add the cornstarch and water combination and stir continuously until the sauce thickens. After it thickens, take it off the stove and let it cool somewhat.
3. Heat the vegetable oil in the fondue pot to 375°F (190°C), using the deep-fry thermometer to ensure the correct temperature.
4. Season the pork cubes with salt and pepper and roll them in the all-purpose flour until completely coated while the oil is heating.
5. Using the fondue forks, carefully dip the flour-coated pork pieces into the hot oil, cooking in batches to avoid overcrowding. Cook for about 3-4 minutes or until golden and cooked through.
6. Once cooked, let the pork chunks cool on a dish covered with paper towels so that any excess oil may be absorbed.
7. With the heated sweet and sour sauce available for dipping, serve right away.
8. If desired, sprinkle with sesame seeds and thinly sliced green onions.

Rosemary Lamb Kebab Fondue

 4 SERVINGS 30 MINUTES 10 MINUTES

Savor the succulence of lamb kebabs infused with aromatic rosemary and spices, all cooked to perfection in a communal oil fondue. Ideal for gatherings, watch the tender morsels sizzle and enjoy a culinary experience that's both interactive and immensely satisfying.

Equipment: Fondue pot, skewers, slotted spoon

Ingredients:

- 1 pound of boneless lamb shoulder or legs, diced into 1-inch pieces
- 2 tbsp fresh rosemary leaves, finely chopped
- 2 garlic cloves, minced
- 1/2 tsp ground cumin
- 1/4 tsp ground coriander
- 1/4 tsp smoked paprika
- Salt and freshly ground black pepper should be added to taste.
- Vegetable oil, for fondue pot
- Assorted dipping sauces (e.g., tzatziki, mint yogurt sauce, or harissa)

Nutritional Information: Calories: 310, Protein: 24g, Carbohydrates: 1g, Fat: 24g, Fiber: 0.5g, Cholesterol: 80 mg, Sodium: 75 mg, Potassium: 330 mg

Directions:

1. In a bowl, mix together the lamb cubes with rosemary, garlic, cumin, coriander, smoked paprika, salt, and pepper until well coated. Let the mixture marinate for at least 20 minutes at room temperature or refrigerate for up to 2 hours for a deeper flavor.
2. Heat the fondue pot on the stovetop to 375°F (190°C) after adding about half of the vegetable oil to it. After the oil reaches the proper temperature, carefully move the pot to the dining table's fondue burner. Please ensure safety measures are in place and instruct your guests on careful use.
3. Thread the marinated lamb onto skewers, with about 3 to 4 pieces per skewer.
4. Allow each visitor to grill their lamb kebabs on skewers in the heated oil for two to three minutes, depending on preferred doneness, or until browned and cooked through.
5. The skewers can be carefully taken out of the oil with a slotted spoon, letting any extra oil fall off.
6. Serve immediately with assorted dipping sauces on the side.

Sea Salt and Vinegar Potato Fondue

 4 SERVINGS   15 MINUTES   5 MINUTES

Experience a tantalizing twist on fondue with our Sea Salt and Vinegar Potato Fondue. Perfectly crispy potato pieces are ready to be dipped into a bubbly hot oil, providing a crunchy exterior and soft, fluffy interior with a zesty vinegar finish. Ideal for sharing and dipping with friends and family, it's a savory treat that turns the classic fondue experience on its head with its mouthwatering flavor profile.

Equipment: Fondue Pot, Skewers or Fondue Forks, Slotted Spoon, Paper Towels

Ingredients:

- Peanut or Canola Oil for frying
- Peel and chop two large russet potatoes into bite-sized chunks.
- 1/4 cup white vinegar
- Salt to taste (sea salt preferred)
- 2 tbsp malt vinegar powder (optional for dusting)

Nutritional Information: Calories: (Amount varies depending on oil absorption), Protein: 3g, Carbohydrates: 37g, Fat: (Amount varies), Fiber: 2.9g, Cholesterol: 0 mg, Sodium: 95 mg, Potassium: 888 mg"

Directions:

1. Fill your fondue pot with the oil of your choice, making sure not to fill more than 1/2 of the pot to prevent spillages. Heat the oil to 375°F or 190°C .
2. Rinse the cut potatoes with water to remove excess starch and then dry thoroughly with paper towels to prevent splattering during frying.
3. Toss the cubed potatoes with the white vinegar and let them sit for a couple of minutes to absorb the flavor.
4. Gently drop the potatoes covered in vinegar into the heated oil in batches, and cook for 4–5 minutes, or until they are crispy and golden brown.
5. Place the potatoes on paper towels to drain after removing them with a slotted spoon. While still hot, sprinkle generously with sea salt, and if available, dust with malt vinegar powder for that extra tang.
6. Skewer the potato cubes with fondue forks and dip them into the hot oil until crispy. For the finest flavor and texture, serve right away.

Honey Mustard Pretzel Chicken Fondue

 4 SERVINGS   20 MINUTES   10 MINUTES

Indulge in a savory twist on fondue with our Honey Mustard Pretzel Chicken, made with tender chicken pieces coated in a crispy, flavorful pretzel crust, paired with a tangy honey mustard dip. It's the ideal balance of crunchy, savory, and sweet, and it will make a big impression at any event.

Equipment: Fondue pot, Skewers or fondue forks, Medium bowl, Plate

Ingredients:

- One pound of skinless, boneless chicken breasts, diced into bite-sized pieces
- 2 cups Pretzels, crushed into fine crumbs
- 1/4 cup Dijon mustard
- 1/4 cup Honey
- 2 tbsp Mayonnaise
- 1 tbsp Apple cider vinegar
- 1 tsp Garlic powder
- 1/2 tsp Paprika
- Salt and pepper, to taste
- Vegetable oil, for frying

Nutritional Information: Calories: 410, Protein: 25g, Carbohydrates: 31g, Fat: 20g, Fiber: 1g, Cholesterol: 65 mg, Sodium: 610 mg, Potassium: 210 mg

Directions:

1. In the fondue pot, heat the vegetable oil to 375°F (190°C) over medium heat.
2. The honey mustard dipping sauce can be made by combining the Dijon mustard, honey, mayonnaise, apple cider vinegar, garlic powder, paprika, salt, and pepper in a medium-sized bowl while the oil is heated. Before serving, set it aside.
3. Place crushed pretzels on a plate. Lightly season the chicken cubes with salt and pepper.
4. Skewer the chicken pieces with the fondue forks.
5. Roll each skewered chicken piece in the crushed pretzels until well coated.
6. When the oil reaches the right temperature, the internal temperature of the chicken should be 165°F (74°C). Gently drop the pretzel-coated chicken pieces into the oil and fry for three to four minutes, or until golden brown and cooked through.
7. After taking the chicken pieces out of the pan, drain any excess oil by letting them sit on a plate covered with paper towels.
8. Serve the fried chicken skewers immediately with the honey mustard dipping sauce.

Old Bay Seafood Fondue

 4 SERVINGS 20 MINUTES 15 MINUTES

Dive into a coastal flavor experience with this Old Bay Seafood Fondue, blending the rich traditions of fondue with the zesty, iconic spice blend loved by seafood enthusiasts. Perfect for entertaining or a special family meal, this homage to the Chesapeake Bay will have everyone dipping and savoring to the last morsel.

Equipment: Fondue pot, Forks or skewers, Stovetop

Ingredients:

- 1 quart peanut or canola oil
- 1 lb mixed seafood (shrimp, scallops, white fish), cut into bite-sized pieces
- 1/2 cup flour
- 2 tbsp Old Bay seasoning
- 1 tsp garlic powder
- 1 lemon, for garnish
- Fresh parsley, for garnish

Nutritional Information: Calories: 390, Protein: 30g, Carbohydrates: 10g, Fat: 25g, Fiber: 1g, Cholesterol: 180 mg, Sodium: 750 mg, Potassium: 280 mg

Directions:

1. Preheat your fondue pot to 375°F (190°C), adding the peanut or canola oil to the fondue pot and allow it to heat fully. A candy thermometer may be used for precise temperature control.
2. While the oil is heating, thoroughly mix the flour, Old Bay seasoning, and garlic powder in a medium bowl. Coat the seafood pieces evenly with the seasoned flour mixture.
3. Once the oil has reached the correct temperature, use fondue forks or skewers to carefully dip the seafood pieces into the hot oil. Cook each piece for 2-4 minutes or until the seafood is golden brown and cooked through. Be sure to cook in small batches to maintain the oil temperature.
4. Carefully remove the cooked seafood from the oil, allowing any excess to drip off, and place them on a plate lined with paper towels to absorb extra oil.
5. As a garnish, include some freshly squeezed lemon juice and fresh parsley.
6. Serve hot with your preferred dipping sauces, including cocktail sauce, tartar sauce, or lemon juice for extra flavor.

Tandoori Vegetable Skewer Fondue

 4 SERVINGS 25 MINUTES 15 MINUTES

Dive into the aromatic world of Indian spices with these sizzling Tandoori Vegetable Skewer Fondues. Robust flavors of tandoori masala married with an assortment of fresh vegetables create a delectably spicy treat to dip in hot oil. Perfect for those who love to add a bit of spice to their comfort food indulgences.

Equipment: Fondue pot, Skewers, Mixing bowl

Ingredients:

- 1 cup Greek yogurt
- 2 tbsp tandoori masala
- 1 tsp garam masala
- 1 tbsp ginger garlic paste
- 2 tbsp lemon juice
- Salt to taste
- Assorted vegetables (bell peppers, onions, zucchini, mushrooms), cut into bite-sized chunks
- Oil for frying (peanut, vegetable or canola)

Nutritional Information: Calories: 180, Protein: 6g, Carbohydrates: 15g, Fat: 9g, Fiber: 3g, Cholesterol: 3 mg, Sodium: 56 mg, Potassium: 250 mg

Directions:

1. Combine the Greek yogurt, lemon juice, ginger garlic paste, garam masala, tandoori masala, and salt in a mixing bowl to make the marinade.
2. Toss the bite-sized chunks of assorted vegetables in the marinade until well coated. Let them marinate for at least 15 minutes. For a deeper flavor, marinate for an hour in the refrigerator.
3. Preheat the oil in the fondue pot to 375°F (190°C). While the oil is heating, thread the marinated vegetables onto skewers.
4. The veggie skewers should be carefully lowered into the fondue pot once the oil is heated. Cook for about 3-5 minutes or until crisp and beautifully charred.
5. After taking the skewers out of the oil, allow the extra oil to drip into paper towels.
6. Serve hot, accompanied by dipping sauces like mint-coriander chutney or cucumber raita.

Korean BBQ Fondue

 6 SERVINGS 15 MINUTES 15 MINUTES

Experience the savory delight of Korean BBQ in a fun and interactive fondue form. This dish calls for soft beef or pig slices to be dipped in a mixture of sweet pear, sesame oil, and soy sauce. It's perfect for a social gathering where guests can enjoy cooking their own morsels to perfection.

Equipment: Fondue Pot, Meat Thermometer, Fondue Forks, Cutting Board, Knife

Ingredients:

- 1 lb Beef sirloin or pork tenderloin, thinly sliced
- 2 cups Vegetable oil or beef tallow for frying
- Marinade: 1/4 cup Soy sauce, 2 tbsp Brown sugar, 1 tbsp Sesame oil, 3 Cloves garlic, minced; 1/2 Medium pear, grated; 1 tsp Ginger, minced; 2 Green onions, thinly sliced; 1 tsp Gochujang (Korean chili paste) or to taste; 1 tsp Toasted sesame seeds; Salt and pepper to taste
- Dipping sauce: 1/4 cup Soy sauce, 1 tbsp Rice vinegar, 1 tsp Sugar, 1 tsp Sesame oil, Crushed red pepper flakes, 1/2 teaspoon (optional), As a garnish, add chopped green onions and toasted sesame seeds.

Nutritional Information: Calories: 320, Protein: 25g, Carbohydrates: 8g, Fat: 22g (Varies with oil absorption), Fiber: 0.5g, Cholesterol: 68mg, Sodium: 830mg, Potassium: 360mg

Directions:

1. In a bowl, combine all the marinade ingredients; mix until the sugar is dissolved. Place the thinly sliced beef or pork in the marinade, ensuring each piece is coated. To achieve a more powerful flavor, marinate it in the refrigerator for at least an hour or overnight covered with plastic wrap.
2. About 15 minutes before serving, fill the fondue pot with vegetable oil or beef tallow and heat it to 350-375°F (175-190°C). To check the temperature, use a meat thermometer.
3. While the oil is heating, prepare the dipping sauce by combining soy sauce, rice vinegar, sugar, sesame oil, and crushed red pepper flakes in a small bowl. Stir until the sugar dissolves and then garnish with sesame seeds and chopped green onions.
4. Once the oil has reached the right temperature, each guest can spear a slice of marinated beef or pork with a fondue fork and fry it in the hot oil until it reaches their desired level of doneness – usually between 10 to 30 seconds depending on how thinly the meat is sliced.
5. Serve immediately with the prepared dipping sauce on the side.

Parmesan Asparagus Fondue

 4 SERVINGS 15 MINUTES 10 MINUTES

Savor the harmony of crispy asparagus wrapped in a delicate veil of golden, nutty Parmesan. This oil fondue indulgence combines the earthy snap of fresh asparagus with a cheesy crust, perfect for those who love the tingling contrast of textures and flavors.

Equipment: Fondue pot, Long fondue forks or skewers, Paper towels

Ingredients:

- 1 lb Asparagus, trimmed
- 1 cup Grated Parmesan cheese
- 2 cups Panko breadcrumbs
- 2 Large eggs
- 1/2 cup All-purpose flour
- Salt and pepper, to taste
- Vegetable oil, for frying

Nutritional Information: Calories: 295, Protein: 16g, Carbohydrates: 28g, Fat: 14g, Fiber: 3g, Cholesterol: 96 mg, Sodium: 390 mg, Potassium: 257 mg

Directions:

1. Begin by setting your fondue pot over a medium heat source to preheat the vegetable oil to 375°F (190°C), ensuring the pot is filled no more than halfway to prevent spills.
2. In a small bowl, whisk the eggs and put aside while the oil heats up. Combine the grated Parmesan and Panko breadcrumbs in another shallow dish, and place the flour seasoned with salt and pepper in a third dish to create a breading station.
3. Roll each asparagus spear in the flour mixture, ensuring it is lightly coated. Dip the floured asparagus in the whisked eggs, allowing excess to drip off.
4. Press the egg-dipped asparagus into the Parmesan breadcrumb mixture, coating it thoroughly for that irresistible crunch.
5. Once the oil has reached the correct temperature, use the fondue forks to carefully lower the breaded asparagus into the hot oil. Fry the asparagus in batches to avoid overcrowding, which can lead to a drop in temperature and soggy outcomes.
6. Fry each batch until golden brown, approximately 3 to 4 minutes, then transfer to paper towels to drain excess oil.
7. Serve immediately for the best texture, accompanied by your favorite dips or dressings for added flavor.

Maple Bacon Brussels Sprout Fondue

 4 SERVINGS   20 MINUTES   10 MINUTES

Experience the savory delight of maple bacon combined with the fresh, earthy tones of Brussels sprouts in a fondue setting. This unique dish takes the traditional fondue concept and spins it with an infusion of smoked bacon flavors and a sweet maple twist, perfect for those who love a robust taste experience.

Equipment: Fondue pot, Forks or skewers for dipping, Chef's knife, Cutting board

Ingredients:

- 1 lb Brussels sprouts, trimmed and halved
- 6 slices thick-cut bacon, chopped into bite-size pieces
- 1/4 cup maple syrup
- 2 cups vegetable oil, or more as needed for the fondue pot.
- 1 teaspoon smoked paprika
- Salt and pepper to taste
- Optional for serving: crusty bread cubes, cherry tomatoes, mushroom caps

Nutritional Information: Calories: 495, Protein: 10g, Carbohydrates: 23g, Fat: 43g, Fiber: 4g, Cholesterol: 22 mg, Sodium: 472 mg, Potassium: 487 mg

Directions:

1. Preheat your fondue pot to the manufacturer's recommended temperature for oil fondue.
2. Cook the bacon bits in a pan over medium heat until crisp. To soak any excess fat, transfer the bacon to a dish lined with paper towels.
3. In the remaining bacon grease, add the halved Brussels sprouts. Season with smoked paprika, salt, and pepper. Sauté them until they are caramelized and tender. This should take about 7-8 minutes.
4. Drizzle the Brussels sprouts with maple syrup, stirring to coat evenly. Cook for an additional 2 minutes until the syrup becomes sticky and the sprouts are well coated.
5. Transfer the cooked bacon and Brussels sprouts to a serving dish.
6. Check the oil temperature in the fondue pot. It should be around 350-375°F. If it's not hot enough, heat it some more until it reaches the right temperature.
7. Using fondue forks or skewers, dip the maple-glazed Brussels sprouts and cooked bacon into the hot oil. Let them fry for 2 to 3 minutes until they become crispy and golden brown. Be sure not to crowd the fondue pot.
8. Serve immediately with the optional crusty bread cubes, cherry tomatoes, and mushroom caps for a complete fondue experience.

Greek Lamb Meatball Fondue

 4 SERVINGS   30 MINUTES   15 MINUTES

Indulge in the flavors of Greece with this mouth-watering Greek Lamb Meatball Fondue. Perfectly seasoned lamb meatballs are cooked to delectable perfection in a sizzling oil fondue. Immerse yourself in the aroma of Mediterranean spices as you enjoy a sociable and delicious dining experience, perfect for any occasion.

Equipment: Fondue pot, Forks or skewers for dipping, Mixing bowl

Ingredients:

- 1 lb Ground lamb
- 1/4 cup Breadcrumbs, ideally panko for a lighter texture
- 1 Large egg
- 2 Cloves garlic, minced
- 1 tbsp Fresh mint, finely chopped
- 1 tbsp Fresh oregano, finely chopped
- 1 tsp Ground cumin
- 1 tsp Paprika
- Salt and pepper to taste
- Vegetable oil for fondue
- 1 Lemon, cut into wedges, for serving
- Tzatziki sauce for dipping

Nutritional Information: Calories: 310, Protein: 19g, Carbohydrates: 6g, Fat: 23g (varies with absorption during frying), Fiber: 1g, Cholesterol: 96 mg, Sodium: 123 mg, Potassium: 249 mg

Directions:

1. In a mixing bowl, combine the ground lamb, breadcrumbs, egg, garlic, mint, oregano, cumin, paprika, salt, and pepper. Blend thoroughly until all components are dispersed equally.
2. Roll the mixture into small, bite-sized meatballs, about an inch in diameter.
3. In the fondue pot, heat the oil over medium heat until it reaches around 375°F (190°C). It's important to maintain a steady temperature for the best cooking results.
4. Once the oil is heated, skewer each meatball with a fondue fork and carefully lower it into the hot oil. Do not overcrowd the fondue pot; cook the meatballs in batches if necessary.
5. Cook the meatballs for about 4-5 minutes or until they are browned on the outside and fully cooked on the inside. Use a meat thermometer to ensure they've reached a safe internal temperature of 160°F (71°C).
6. After cooking, take the meatballs out of the oil and place them on a plate covered with paper towels to drain.
7. Serve the meatballs hot with lemon wedges and tzatziki sauce for dipping.

Tex-Mex Queso Fundido Fondue

 6 SERVINGS 15 MINUTES 10 MINUTES

Dive into the zesty world of Tex-Mex cuisine with this Queso Fundido Fondue, a delightful blend of creamy melted cheese and bold spices. Perfect for dipping your favorite tortilla chips, vegetables, or meats, this fondue is a decadent, interactive meal that will ignite your taste buds and bring the fiesta to your table.

Equipment: Fondue pot, Stove, Fondue forks or skewers

Ingredients:

- 1 lb Sharp cheddar cheese, shredded
- 1/2 lb Monterey Jack cheese, shredded
- 1 cup Lager beer or chicken broth
- 1 tbsp Cornstarch
- 1 medium Tomato, seeded and diced
- 1/4 cup Onion, finely chopped
- 1 Green bell pepper, diced
- 1 Jalapeño pepper, seeded and minced (adjust to taste)
- 2 cloves Garlic, minced
- 1 tsp Ground cumin
- 1/2 tsp Smoked paprika
- 1/4 cup Cilantro, freshly chopped
- Salt and pepper to taste

Nutritional Information: Calories: 350, Protein: 22g, Carbohydrates: 5g, Fat: 26g, Fiber: 0.5g, Cholesterol: 70 mg, Sodium: 530 mg, Potassium: 70 mg

Directions:

1. In a bowl, toss the shredded cheeses with the cornstarch to coat evenly. This helps in thickening and prevents the cheese from clumping.
2. Place the chicken broth or lager beer in the fondue pot and heat it to a low simmer over medium heat. Be careful not to let it boil to avoid curdling the cheese.
3. Stirring frequently with a wooden spoon, gradually add the cheese and cornstarch mixture until the cheeses are completely melted and the mixture is smooth.
4. Once the cheese is melted, add the diced tomato, onion, green bell pepper, jalapeño, garlic, cumin, and smoked paprika. Stir well to combine.
5. Cook for an additional 3-5 minutes, continuing to stir, until the fondue is hot and ingredients are well incorporated. Add more salt and pepper to taste when seasoning.
6. Sprinkle with freshly chopped cilantro just before serving. Keep the fondue pot over a low flame to maintain its smooth texture.
7. Serve immediately with tortilla chips, fresh vegetables, or cooked meats for dipping.

Moroccan Spiced Carrot Fondue

 4 SERVINGS 15 MINUTES 10 MINUTES

Dive into an aromatic encounter with this Moroccan Spiced Carrot Fondue, where the sweetness of carrots meets a warm symphony of Moroccan spices. Perfect for dipping savory meats and veggies, this dish will transport your senses to the fragrant streets of Marrakesh.

Equipment: Fondue pot, Spiralizer or grater, Cutting board, Kitchen knife, Mixing bowl

Ingredients:

- 1 tablespoon Olive oil
- 4 cups Carrots, peeled and spiralized or grated
- 1 teaspoon Ground cumin
- 1 teaspoon Sweet paprika
- 1/4 teaspoon Ground cinnamon
- 1/8 teaspoon Cayenne pepper (adjust to heat preference)
- 1/2 teaspoon Salt
- 1/4 teaspoon Black pepper
- 2 cups Vegetable broth
- 2 tablespoons Honey
- 1 tablespoon Fresh lemon juice
- 2 tablespoons Fresh cilantro, finely chopped
- 1 tablespoon Sesame seeds (optional, for garnish)

Nutritional Information: Calories: 175, Protein: 2g, Carbohydrates: 31g, Fat: 5g, Fiber: 6g, Cholesterol: 0 mg, Sodium: 800 mg, Potassium: 497 mg

Directions:

1. In the fondue pot, heat the olive oil over medium heat. Add the spiralized/grated carrots and cook until they start to soften, for about 5 minutes.
2. Stir in cumin, paprika, cinnamon, cayenne pepper, salt, and black pepper. Cook for another 2-3 minutes to toast the spices and coat the carrots evenly.
3. Gradually pour in the vegetable broth while continuing to stir, ensuring a smooth texture.
4. Bring the mixture to a simmer and let it cook for another 3 minutes, allowing the flavors to meld.
5. Drizzle honey over the mixture and stir in the fresh lemon juice to enhance the flavors. Adjust seasoning if necessary.
6. Just before serving, sprinkle the fresh cilantro over the fondue and garnish with sesame seeds, if desired.
7. Keep the flame under the fondue pot low to maintain the temperature without overcooking the fondue.

Sichuan Spicy Tofu Fondue

 4 SERVINGS   20 MINUTES   10 MINUTES

Dive into the heart of Sichuan cuisine with this spicy tofu fondue, perfect for those who crave the heat and distinct numbing sensation characteristic of Sichuan peppercorns. This bold fondue brings the allure of Chinese flavors directly to your dinner table, making for a zesty alternative to traditional fondue recipes.

Equipment: Fondue pot, Fondue forks or skewers, Stove

Ingredients:

- Cut 1 pound of firm tofu into 1-inch cubes after draining.
- Two cups of vegetable or peanut oil for frying
- 3 tbsp Sichuan peppercorns
- 2 cloves Garlic, finely minced
- 2 inch Fresh ginger, peeled and grated
- 4 tbsp Doubanjiang (Sichuan chili bean paste)
- 2 tbsp Soy sauce
- 1 tbsp Sesame oil
- 1 tsp Sugar
- 2 Spring onions, thinly sliced for garnish
- Fresh cilantro leaves, for garnish

Nutritional Information: Calories: 390, Protein: 13g, Carbohydrates: 5g, Fat: 36g, Fiber: 1g, Cholesterol: 0 mg, Sodium: 450 mg, Potassium: 200 mg

Directions:

1. Begin by drying the tofu cubes with paper towels to remove excess moisture. This will prevent splattering when the tofu is submerged in hot oil.
2. To make the oil suitable for deep frying, heat it to approximately 350°F (177°C) in the fondue pot over medium-high heat on the stove.
3. Add a few tofu cubes to the oil at a time, using fondue forks or skewers. Fry the tofu until it's golden and crispy, approximately 2–3 minutes, then remove and drain on paper towels.
4. In a separate small bowl, mix together Sichuan peppercorns, minced garlic, grated ginger, Doubanjiang, soy sauce, sesame oil, and sugar to create the dipping sauce.
5. Arrange the cooked tofu on a serving platter. Garnish with sliced spring onions and fresh cilantro leaves.
6. Serve the crispy tofu alongside the spicy Sichuan sauce for dipping.
7. Guests can use their fondue forks or skewers to dip the tofu into the sauce, enjoying the spicy, numbing, and savory flavors.

Caribbean Jerk Chicken Fondue

 4 SERVINGS   20 MINUTES   15 MINUTES

Immerse your senses in the bold flavors of the Caribbean with this Jerk Chicken Fondue recipe. Tender chunks of chicken are marinated in a spicy, aromatic jerk sauce and then cooked to perfection in sizzling oil, offering a tantalizing aroma and a fiery flavor that will excite your palate and transport you straight to a tropical island.

Equipment: Fondue Pot, Forks for Dipping, Mixing Bowl

Ingredients:

- One pound of chicken breast, sliced into small pieces
- Two cups of frying oil, either canola or peanut
- Jerk Marinade: 1/4 cup Soy Sauce; 2 tbsp Lime Juice; 3 Green Onions, chopped; 1 Garlic Clove, minced; 1 Scotch Bonnet Pepper, finely chopped (remove seeds for less heat); 1 tbsp Brown Sugar; 1 tsp Ground Allspice; 1 tsp Dried Thyme; 1/2 tsp Cinnamon; 1/2 tsp Ground Nutmeg; 1/2 tsp Ground Ginger; Salt and Pepper, to taste;
- Dipping Sauce: 1/2 cup Mango Chutney; 1 tbsp Fresh Lime Juice; 1/2 tsp Grated Ginger

Nutritional Information: Calories: 310, Protein: 26g, Carbohydrates: 15g, Fat: 16g (based on oil absorption), Fiber: 1g, Cholesterol: 65 mg, Sodium: 520 mg, Potassium: 290 mg

Directions:

1. Combine soy sauce, lime juice, green onions, garlic, Scotch bonnet pepper, brown sugar, allspice, thyme, cinnamon, nutmeg, ginger, salt, and pepper in a mixing bowl to create the jerk marinade.
2. Toss the chicken pieces in the marinade to ensure even coating. For maximum flavor intensity, marinate the dish in the refrigerator for at least an hour, but better overnight. Cover the bowl.
3. Prior to cooking, bring the marinated chicken to room temperature for even cooking.
4. In your fondue pot, heat the oil to 350°F. Use a thermometer to ensure the oil is at the correct temperature for safe and accurate cooking.
5. While the oil is heating, prepare the dipping sauce by combining the mango chutney, lime juice, and grated ginger in a small bowl. Set aside.
6. Once the oil is hot, use fondue forks to dip the marinated chicken pieces into the oil. Cook for 3-6 minutes or until the chicken is golden brown and cooked through.
7. Serve the cooked chicken with the prepared mango chutney dipping sauce.

Mediterranean Falafel Fondue

 4 SERVINGS 25 MINUTES 5 MINUTES

Immerse yourself into the flavors of the Mediterranean with this innovative Falafel Fondue. Crisp, herby falafel balls are perfect for dipping into a silky, richly spiced oil fondue. Enjoy the delightful contrast of a crunchy exterior giving way to a warm, soft interior, coupled with the interactive fun of fondue dining. Perfect for a social gathering or a family meal, this dish brings a twist to the traditional fondue experience.

Equipment: Fondue pot, Fondue forks or skewers, Deep frying pan or fryer

Ingredients:

- 2 cups Chickpeas, soaked overnight and drained
- 1 large Onion, finely chopped
- 4 cloves Garlic, minced
- 1 cup Fresh parsley, finely chopped
- 1 cup Fresh cilantro, finely chopped
- 2 tsp Ground cumin
- 1 tsp Ground coriander
- 1 tsp Salt
- 1/2 tsp Ground black pepper
- 1/2 tsp Cayenne pepper (optional for extra spice)
- 1 tsp Baking soda
- 4 cups Vegetable oil (for frying)
- Optional dips: Tahini sauce, tzatziki, or a spicy harissa dip

Nutritional Information: Calories: 300, Protein: 9g, Carbohydrates: 35g, Fat: 15g, Fiber: 9g, Cholesterol: 0mg,

Directions:

1. In a food processor, onion, combine chickpeas, garlic, parsley, cilantro, cumin, coriander, salt, black pepper, and cayenne pepper. Process until mixture is coarsely ground.
2. Transfer mixture to a bowl and stir in baking soda. Let it rest for 15 minutes. This allows the flavors to meld and the baking soda to help in creating a fluffy texture.
3. Shape the mixture into small balls or slightly flattened discs about the size of a walnut.
4. Heat the vegetable oil in the deep frying pan or fryer to 350°F (175°C). Ensure the oil is at least an inch deep to allow for proper frying.
5. Once the oil reaches the proper temperature, use fondue forks or skewers to dip the falafel balls into the hot oil. Fry in batches until falafel is golden brown, usually about 3-5 minutes.
6. Use a slotted spoon or similar tool to remove the falafels from the oil and let them drain on a paper towel-lined plate.
7. Set the fondue pot over a flame to keep the oil warm for dipping if desired. Guests can skewer their own falafel balls and dip into the oil to re-crisp or keep them warm as they eat.

Japanese Katsu Fondue

 4 SERVINGS 20 MINUTES 15 MINUTES

Dive into the crispy satisfaction of Japanese Katsu Fondue, an indulgent twist on traditional oil fondue that pairs the crunch of panko-crusted proteins with a velvety soy and mirin dipping sauce. Perfect for those who love the fusion of Eastern flavors and communal dining.

Equipment: Fondue pot, Skewers or fondue forks, Paper towels

Ingredients:

- 1 quart Vegetable oil (for frying)
- 1 lb Chicken breast or pork cutlets, sliced into strips
- 1 cup All-purpose flour
- 2 large Eggs, beaten
- 2 cups Panko breadcrumbs
- Salt and pepper, to taste
- 1/4 cup Soy sauce (for dipping sauce)
- 1/4 cup Mirin (for dipping sauce)
- 1 tsp Sugar (for dipping sauce)
- 1/2 tsp Grated ginger (for dipping sauce)

Nutritional Information: Calories: 620, Protein: 35g, Carbohydrates: 52g, Fat: 30g, Fiber: 2g, Cholesterol: 180 mg, Sodium: 910 mg, Potassium: 400 mg

Directions:

1. Begin by heating the vegetable oil in the fondue pot over medium-high heat, aiming for a temperature of 375°F (190°C).
2. Season the chicken or pork strips with salt and pepper. Dredge each strip in flour, shaking off the excess, then dip into the beaten eggs, and finally coat them generously with the panko breadcrumbs.
3. When the oil is hot, use skewers or fondue forks to carefully lower the breaded strips into the oil. Cook for 3 to 4 minutes or until golden brown and cooked through. Do this in batches to avoid overcrowding, which can lower the oil temperature.
4. Prepare the dipping sauce while the meat cooks by combining soy sauce, mirin, sugar, and grated ginger in a small bowl and stirring until the sugar dissolves.
5. Once cooked, transfer the katsu strips to a plate lined with paper towels to drain any excess oil.
6. Serve the crispy katsu strips with the soy-mirin dipping sauce on the side.

German Schnitzel Fondue

 6 SERVINGS   30 MINUTES   10 MINUTES

Dive into the flavors of Germany with this delectable German Schnitzel Fondue. An indulgent oil fondue recipe that combines tender veal, seasoned breadcrumbs, and satisfying dips for an interactive dining experience perfect for gatherings or a special family dinner.

Equipment: Fondue Pot, Meat Thermometer, Forks or Skewers, Paper Towels

Ingredients:

- 1 lb Veal cutlets, tenderized and cut into bite-size pieces
- 2 Cups Bread crumbs, seasoned with salt, pepper, and paprika
- 2 Large Eggs, beaten
- 1 Cup Flour, for dredging
- Oil for frying, such as canola or peanut, enough to fill the fondue pot 1/2 way
- Salt and Pepper, to taste
- Lemon wedges, for serving
- Assorted dipping sauces, such as horseradish cream, mustard, and aioli

Nutritional Information: Calories: 490, Protein: 28g, Carbohydrates: 22g, Fat: 30g, Fiber: 1g, Cholesterol: 142 mg, Sodium: 200 mg, Potassium: 400 mg

Directions:

1. Begin by setting up your fondue pot on a heatproof surface and fill it halfway with frying oil suitable for high heat. Heat the oil to 375°F (190°C), using a meat thermometer to monitor the temperature.
2. While the oil is heating, prepare the schnitzel bites. Season the veal cutlets with salt and pepper, cut into bite-sized pieces if not already done, and set aside.
3. Organize your dredging station by placing flour on a plate or shallow bowl, beaten eggs in another, and seasoned breadcrumbs in a third.
4. Dredge each piece of veal first in flour, shaking off any excess. Dip next into the beaten eggs, ensuring it's fully coated. Finally, coat thoroughly with the seasoned breadcrumbs.
5. Once the oil has reached the correct temperature, spear a breaded veal piece with a fondue fork or skewer and carefully submerge it into the hot oil.
6. Fry each piece for about 3 to 4 minutes until golden brown and cooked through. The meat's internal temperature should reach 145°F (63°C).
7. Remove the cooked schnitzel bites from the oil and let them rest on paper towels to absorb any excess oil.
8. Serve hot alongside lemon wedges for squeezing and a variety of dipping sauces for an authentic touch.

Southern Fried Green Tomato Fondue

 6 SERVINGS   25 MINUTES   10 MINUTES

Experience the charm of the south with this crispy and tangy Southern Fried Green Tomato Fondue, perfect for dipping in an oil fondue. The fusion of the rich batter and the slight tartness of green tomatoes creates an indulgent twist on classic southern fare, elevating your fondue night to an unforgettable culinary adventure.

Equipment: Deep Fryer or Heavy Pot, Thermometer, Paper Towels, Slotted Spoon

Ingredients:

- 4 medium Green Tomatoes, sliced into 1/2-inch thick rounds
- 2 cups All-Purpose Flour
- 1 cup Cornmeal
- 1 tablespoon Garlic Powder
- 1 tablespoon Paprika
- 1 teaspoon Cayenne Pepper
- 2 Large Eggs
- 1/4 cup Buttermilk
- Salt and Pepper to taste
- Oil for frying (Peanut or canola oil works well)

Nutritional Information: Calories: 355, Protein: 9g, Carbohydrates: 47g, Fat: 15g (varies based on oil absorption during frying), Fiber: 4g, Cholesterol: 62 mg, Sodium: 238 mg, Potassium: 354 mg

Directions:

1. Begin by setting up the deep fryer or heavy pot. Pour enough oil to come halfway up the sides of the pot, and heat to 375°F (190°C). Use the thermometer to monitor the oil temperature.
2. Pat dry the green tomato slices with paper towels to remove excess moisture; this step is crucial for the batter to stick properly.
3. In a shallow bowl, whisk together the flour, cornmeal, garlic powder, paprika, cayenne pepper, salt, and pepper.
4. Beat the eggs and buttermilk together in a separate dish until they are smooth.
5. Dip each tomato slice first into the flour mixture to coat, then into the egg buttermilk mixture, and then back into the flour mixture to ensure each slice is well-coated.
6. Once the oil has reached the correct temperature, use a slotted spoon to carefully lower the battered tomato slices into the hot oil. Do not overcrowd the pot; fry the tomatoes in batches.
7. Fry for 2 to 3 minutes or until golden brown and crispy. Make sure to turn the slices halfway through frying for even browning.
8. Use the slotted spoon to remove the fried green tomatoes from the oil and drain them on paper towels.
9. Serve hot as part of your oil fondue spread, alongside your favorite dipping sauces such as ranch dressing, remoulade, or spicy aioli.

Decadent Chocolate Fondue Delights

Classic Swiss Chocolate Fondue

 4 SERVINGS 15 MINUTES 10 MINUTES

Savor the decadent richness of Classic Swiss Chocolate Fondue, a beloved treat that will transport your taste senses to the very center of Switzerland. This smooth, velvety concoction combines the creamy textures of authentic Swiss chocolate and heavy cream with a touch of coffee to create a decadent dipping experience perfect for any chocolate lover's dream.

Equipment: Fondue pot, Heat-resistant spatula, Fondue forks

Ingredients:

- 200g High-quality Swiss dark chocolate, chopped
- 1/2 cup Heavy cream
- 2 tbsp Brewed coffee, cooled
- 1 tsp Vanilla extract
- Pinch of salt
- Assorted dippers (such as fresh strawberries, banana slices, marshmallows, pound cake cubes, or wafer cookies)

Nutritional Information: Calories: 500, Protein: 4g, Carbohydrates: 45g, Fat: 35g, Fiber: 5g, Cholesterol: 35 mg, Sodium: 46 mg, Potassium: 330 mg

Directions:

1. In a medium saucepan, simmer the heavy cream over low heat until it starts to steam, being careful not to let it boil. Stir occasionally to avoid burning the cream.
2. When the cream is heated through and the chocolate has melted fully, add the chopped Swiss chocolate and whisk gently until the mixture is smooth.
3. Stir in the cooled brewed coffee, vanilla extract, and a pinch of salt, combining everything until you achieve a glossy, even consistency.
4. Transfer the chocolate blend into the fondue pot and set it over a low flame, or over a candle if you're utilizing a classic fondue set.
5. Arrange your choice of dippers on a platter around the fondue pot.
6. Using fondue forks, dip the assorted fruits, cake cubes, or cookies into the chocolate mixture and enjoy!

Midnight Dark Chocolate & Sea Salt Fondue

 4 SERVINGS 10 MINUTES 5 MINUTES

Dive into the sultry depths of this Midnight Dark Chocolate & Sea Salt Fondue, a captivating blend of bittersweet darkness and the light kiss of sea salt. It's ideal for a decadent get-together or romantic evening, and it's sure to be the talk of the dessert table.

Equipment: Fondue Pot, Heat-Resistant Spatula, Fondue Forks

Ingredients:

- 8 oz Quality Dark Chocolate (70% cacao or higher), finely chopped
- 1/2 cup Heavy Cream
- 1 tbsp Unsalted Butter
- 1 tsp Pure Vanilla Extract
- 1/4 tsp Fine Sea Salt; more for decoration
- Assorted Fondue Dippers (strawberries, banana slices, marshmallows, pound cake cubes, etc.)

Nutritional Information: Calories: 390, Protein: 3g, Carbohydrates: 25g, Fat: 30g, Fiber: 4g, Cholesterol: 45 mg, Sodium: 150 mg, Potassium: 420 mg

Directions:

1. Place the heavy cream in a small saucepan and boil over medium heat until it begins to simmer. Be sure not to let it come to a boil.
2. Add the finely chopped dark chocolate and unsalted butter to the fondue pot. Over the chocolate and butter, pour the warm cream.
3. To soften the chocolate, let the mixture sit for one or two minutes. After that, stir the mixture gradually until the chocolate has melted and the fondue is smooth.
4. Stir in the pure vanilla extract and sea salt until fully incorporated.
5. Place the fondue pot over its flame to keep the chocolate warm and liquid.
6. Arrange your chosen dippers on a platter around the fondue pot.
7. Using fondue forks, dip the assorted items into the warm, velvety chocolate, sprinkling a tiny pinch of sea salt atop before eating for an extra burst of flavor and texture.

White Chocolate Raspberry Swirl Fondue

 4 SERVINGS 10 MINUTES 10 MINUTES

The sharpness of fresh raspberries and the creamy richness of white chocolate come together in this White Chocolate Raspberry Swirl Fondue, creating a symphony of tastes. An indulgent treat that's perfect for dipping fruits, marshmallows, or even chunks of pound cake, this fondue is a visually stunning and irresistible dessert that's as perfect for romantic evenings as it is for entertaining friends.

Equipment: Fondue pot, Heat-proof spatula, Fondue forks or skewers

Ingredients:

- 8 oz White chocolate chips or chopped white chocolate
- 1/2 cup Heavy cream
- 1/3 cup Pure raspberry puree (strained to remove seeds)
- 1 tbsp Orange liqueur or raspberry liqueur (optional)
- Fresh fruit pieces (strawberries, banana slices, apple slices), marshmallows, and pound cake for dipping

Nutritional Information: Calories: 452, Protein: 4g, Carbohydrates: 35g, Fat: 34g, Fiber: 1g, Cholesterol: 31 mg, Sodium: 76 mg, Potassium: 165 mg

Directions:

1. Begin by preparing your raspberry puree, straining out the seeds for a smoother fondue. Set aside.
2. Steam forms when the heavy cream in a medium saucepan is heated over low heat. Do not let it boil to prevent the chocolate from seizing.
3. Stir the white chocolate into the cream gradually while continuing to stir until the chocolate has melted completely and the mixture is smooth.
4. Stir in the orange or raspberry liqueur if you're using it, to enhance the flavor profile of the fondue.
5. Transfer the white chocolate mixture to your fondue pot, keeping the heat low to maintain its smooth texture.
6. Gently swirl in the raspberry puree with a spatula to create beautiful red swirls throughout the fondue. Do not mix completely; the goal is to have streaks of raspberry.
7. Serve right away with a selection of fresh fruit, marshmallows, and small pound cake pieces for dipping. Use fondue forks or skewers for a fun and interactive dessert experience.

Rich Caramel Milk Chocolate Fondue

 6 SERVINGS 15 MINUTES 10 MINUTES

Indulge in the smooth and creamy goodness of our Rich Caramel Milk Chocolate Fondue. Perfectly balanced with velvety milk chocolate and a swirl of luxurious caramel, this fondue is a decadent treat ideal for dipping fruits, marshmallows or your favorite dessert bites. A simple yet sophisticated dessert that's sure to delight all your senses.

Equipment: Fondue Pot, Heat-Resistant Spatula, Fondue Forks

Ingredients:

- 8 oz Milk Chocolate, finely chopped
- 1/2 cup Heavy Cream
- 1/4 cup Caramel Sauce
- 1 tsp Vanilla Extract
- Pinch of sea salt
- Assorted Dippables (strawberries, marshmallows, brownie bites, pretzels, etc.)

Nutritional Information: Calories: 290, Protein: 3g, Carbohydrates: 27g, Fat: 20g, Fiber: 1g, Cholesterol: 22 mg, Sodium: 130 mg, Potassium: 133 mg

Directions:

1. Finely chop the milk chocolate and heavy cream and place them in a heatproof basin. Place the bowl over a pot of simmering water to melt the chocolate, making sure the water does not touch the bottom of the bowl. Stir gently until smooth and well combined.
2. After taking the liquid off the heat, stir in the vanilla extract, caramel sauce, and a small teaspoon of sea salt until it becomes glossy and smooth.
3. Transfer the chocolate-caramel mixture to your fondue pot and keep warm according to the fondue pot's instructions.
4. Arrange your dippables around the fondue pot, each on a separate plate to keep things organized.
5. Spear your chosen dippable with a fondue fork and dip into the Rich Caramel Milk Chocolate Fondue, making sure to get a generous coating of the chocolate-caramel mix.

Spicy Aztec Chocolate Fondue

 6 SERVINGS 10 MINUTES 10 MINUTES

Experience the ancient indulgence with a kick—Spicy Aztec Chocolate Fondue blends the rich, complex flavors of dark chocolate with a spicy cayenne pepper punch, all kissed by the warmth of cinnamon and vanilla. Perfect for those who love a sweet heat.

Equipment: Fondue Pot, Heat-resistant Spatula or Whisk, Measuring Cups and Spoons

Ingredients:

- 1 lb High-quality Dark Chocolate, chopped
- 1 cup Heavy Cream
- 1 tsp Ground Cinnamon
- Half a teaspoon of ground cayenne pepper, or to taste
- One split vanilla bean (or two teaspoons of vanilla extract)
- A pinch of Fine Sea Salt
- Your choice of dippers: strawberries, sliced banana, marshmallows, brownie chunks, pretzels, etc.

Nutritional Information: Calories: 560, Protein: 6g, Carbohydrates: 52g, Fat: 36g, Fiber: 7g, Cholesterol: 35 mg, Sodium: 20 mg, Potassium: 420 mg

Directions:

1. The heavy cream should be warmed in a saucepan over low heat; do not allow it to boil.
2. Add the chopped dark chocolate to the fondue pot, stirring with the spatula or whisk as it begins to melt.
3. Remove the vanilla bean seeds and add them (or the vanilla extract) to the chocolate mixture. To ensure uniform distribution, stir.
4. Add the cayenne, ground cinnamon, and a little teaspoon of sea salt and mix until the chocolate is smooth and well incorporated.
5. Once the chocolate has fully melted and the ingredients are thoroughly blended, transfer the fondue pot to its stand at the dining table. Adjust the flame to keep the fondue warm, not hot.
6. Serve immediately with your favorite dippers arranged around the fondue pot.

Bourbon Vanilla Bean Chocolate Fondue

 6 SERVINGS 15 MINUTES 10 MINUTES

Indulge in the rich, velvety smoothness of this Bourbon Vanilla Bean Chocolate Fondue, where the understated warmth of bourbon and the aromatic allure of vanilla beans meld with the deep, decadent tones of premium chocolate. Designed to be the centerpiece of any gathering, this fondue is a true celebration of taste that combines the complexity of fine flavors in a sumptuous dip that's perfect for fruit, marshmallows, and more.

Equipment: Fondue pot, Whisk, Heatproof bowl

Ingredients:

- 10 oz Semisweet chocolate, chopped
- 1/2 cup Heavy cream
- 2 tbsp Bourbon
- 1 Vanilla bean, split and seeds scraped
- Pinch of Salt
- Assorted items for dipping (strawberries, banana slices, marshmallows, pound cake cubes, etc.)

Nutritional Information: Calories: 330, Protein: 2.9g, Carbohydrates: 25.2g, Fat: 24.1g, Fiber: 3.1g, Cholesterol: 27 mg, Sodium: 17 mg, Potassium: 202 mg

Directions:

1. Pour the heavy cream and chopped chocolate into a heatproof bowl, making sure the bottom of the basin stays over the simmering water.
2. Stir the chocolate and cream mixture gently with the whisk until the chocolate has fully melted and the mixture is smooth.
3. Stir the vanilla bean scraps into the chocolate mixture until well combined, making sure that the fondue has a consistent vanilla flavor.
4. With a dash of salt to counterbalance the sweetness and bring out the flavors of the chocolate and vanilla, whisk the bourbon into the chocolate mixture.
5. Once everything is well combined and the fondue mixture is smooth and glossy, carefully transfer it to the fondue pot set over a gentle flame to keep it warm.
6. Serve the Bourbon Vanilla Bean Chocolate Fondue with your chosen dipping items arranged on a platter around the fondue pot.

Cherry Blossom Chocolate Fondue

 6 SERVINGS   15 MINUTES   10 MINUTES

Immerse yourself in a romantic infusion of cherry and chocolate with this Cherry Blossom Chocolate Fondue. The elegant blend of rich dark chocolate, tart cherry flavors, and a hint of floral notes create a decadent dessert that's perfect for spring gatherings or a cozy night in.

Equipment: Fondue pot, Heatproof Stirring Spoon, Fondue Forks

Ingredients:

- 8 oz Quality Dark Chocolate, chopped
- 1 cup Heavy Cream
- 1/3 cup Cherry Liqueur (e.g., Kirsch or Cherry Brandy)
- 1 tsp Vanilla Extract
- 2 tsp Edible Rose Water
- A pinch of Salt
- Fresh cherries with stems, for dipping
- Chopped nuts, for garnish (optional)

Nutritional Information: Calories: 367, Protein: 3g, Carbohydrates: 25g, Fat: 16g, Fiber: 3g, Cholesterol: 54 mg, Sodium: 17 mg, Potassium: 211 mg

Directions:

1. Set a pan of simmering water over your fondue pot or heatproof bowl to start.
2. Add the heavy cream to the fondue pot and heat until it is warm but not boiling.
3. Gradually whisk in the chopped dark chocolate, and stir until the chocolate melts completely and the mixture smoothes out.
4. Stir in the cherry liqueur, vanilla extract, and edible rose water, mixing well to ensure even distribution of the cherry blossom flavor.
5. To bring out the rich flavors of the chocolate, sprinkle in a little salt.
6. If the consistency is too thick, add a little more cream to reach the desired fluidity for dipping.
7. Once everything is smoothly combined, transfer the mixture to your serving fondue pot that's prepared to keep the fondue warm.
8. Serve with fresh cherries for dipping, and you may also offer a dish of chopped nuts for guests to sprinkle on their cherry-dipped chocolate bites.

Orange Zest and Grand Marnier Fondue

 6 SERVINGS   15 MINUTES   5 MINUTES

Dive into the citrusy allure of this luscious chocolate fondue with a twist of orange and an infusion of Grand Marnier. The perfect blend of creamy chocolate and zesty orange flavor, complemented by the warmth of the liqueur, will turn any gathering into a gourmet experience.

Equipment: Fondue pot, Heat-resistant stirring spatula, Fondue forks or skewers

Ingredients:

- 8 oz. Semi-sweet chocolate, chopped
- 1/2 cup Heavy cream
- 3 tbsp. Grand Marnier liqueur
- 1 tbsp. Orange zest
- 1/4 tsp. Sea salt

Nutritional Information: Calories: Approx. 290, Protein: 2.5g, Carbohydrates: 25g, Fat: 18g, Fiber: 3g, Cholesterol: 27mg, Sodium: 105mg, Potassium: 200mg

Directions:

1. Begin by preparing your dipping items. Wash the fruits and cut them into bite-size pieces; set aside with the marshmallows and cake cubes.
2. Pour in the chopped semi-sweet chocolate and heavy cream to the fondue pot. Gently cook the mixture over low heat, stirring regularly with a heat-resistant spatula, until the chocolate is totally melted and smooth.
3. Stir in the Grand Marnier liqueur and orange zest, and continue to mix well. Allow the mixture to warm through until it is hot without letting it come to a boil.
4. As the mixture heats up and becomes a smooth fondue, season with a pinch of sea salt to enhance the flavors.
5. Once the fondue is ready, lower the flame to keep it warm. You can now begin to dip your assorted fruits, marshmallows, and cake cubes using the fondue forks or skewers.
6. Serve immediately while the fondue is warm and velvety.

Peppermint Patty Chocolate Fondue

 8 SERVINGS 15 MINUTES 10 MINUTES

Enjoy a refreshing spin on a classic chocolate fondue with our Peppermint Patty Chocolate Fondue. Dark chocolate and peppermint unite in a delectable melt, infusing each dipped fruit or cake piece with the vibrant taste of a peppermint patty. This fondue is ideal for a festive event or a relaxing night in, and it will delight mint-chocolate enthusiasts.

Equipment: Fondue pot, Heatproof bowl (if melting chocolate via double boiler method), Small saucepan

Ingredients:
- 8 ounces of high-quality dark chocolate, chopped
- 1/2 cup heavy cream
- 1/4 cup milk
- 3 tablespoons unsalted butter
- 2 tablespoons sugar
- 1/2 teaspoon pure vanilla extract
- 1/8 teaspoon salt
- 4-5 drops peppermint extract (or to taste)

Nutritional Information: Calories: 270, Protein: 2g, Carbohydrates: 18g, Fat: 22g, Fiber: 2g, Cholesterol: 31 mg, Sodium: 58 mg, Potassium: 158 mg

Directions:
1. Combine the dark chocolate, heavy cream, milk, butter, sugar, vanilla extract, and salt in the fondue pot or a heatproof bowl set over a pot of simmering water (double boiler method).
2. Stir constantly until the chocolate has melted and the ingredients are well blended into a creamy consistency.
3. Once smooth, stir in the peppermint extract. Begin by adding a few drops, then adjust to taste.
4. Transfer the bowl to the fondue pot if you used a double boiler method.
5. Carefully light the burner under the fondue pot to keep the mixture warm, ensuring it doesn't boil. Stir occasionally to prevent sticking or burning.
6. Serve immediately with an assortment of fondue dippers such as strawberries, banana slices, marshmallows, biscotti, or pound cake cubes.

Smoky Bacon Chocolate Fondue

 8 SERVINGS 15 MINUTES 10 MINUTES

Experience the tantalizing combination of rich chocolate heightened by the savory notes of crispy bacon in this Smoky Bacon Chocolate Fondue. The perfect blend of sweet and salty, it's an unexpected twist on a classic treat that's sure to delight your taste buds.

Equipment: Fondue pot, Whisk, Heat-resistant spatula

Ingredients:
- 8 oz Semi-sweet chocolate, chopped
- 3/4 cup Heavy cream
- 1/2 tsp Smoked paprika
- 1 tbsp Bourbon or whiskey (optional)
- 6 strips Bacon, cooked crispy and finely chopped
- Pinch Sea salt or fleur de sel

Nutritional Information: Calories: 310, Protein: 3g, Carbohydrates: 16g, Fat: 24g, Fiber: 1g, Cholesterol: 40 mg, Sodium: 150 mg, Potassium: 180 mg

Directions:
1. Begin by cooking the bacon until it is crispy. Drain it on paper towels, and once cooled, chop finely.
2. Place the heavy cream in the fondue pot and heat gently until it starts to warm, being careful not to boil.
3. Slowly whisk in the semi-sweet chocolate into the warm cream until the mixture becomes smooth.
4. Add the smoked paprika and, if you're using it, the bourbon or whiskey into the chocolate mixture, stirring well to ensure it is fully incorporated.
5. Stir in half of the finely chopped crispy bacon into the chocolate mixture, retaining the rest for garnish.
6. Once everything is well combined and the fondue is smooth, sprinkle a pinch of sea salt or fleur de sel to enhance the flavors.
7. To serve, garnish the top with the rest of the crispy bacon and surround the fondue pot with your choice of dippers.

Hazelnut Espresso Fondue

 4 SERVINGS 15 MINUTES 10 MINUTES

Indulge in the creamy, nutty flavors of our Hazelnut Espresso Fondue, where the rich aroma of espresso meets the velvety taste of chocolate and the toasted warmth of hazelnuts. This luxurious concoction is perfect for dipping your favorite fruits, cakes, and marshmallows, providing an exquisite ending to any meal or a sophisticated centerpiece for a gathering of friends and family.

Equipment: Fondue pot, Heatproof stirring utensil, Fondue forks or skewers

Ingredients:

- 8 oz High-quality semi-sweet chocolate, chopped
- 1/2 cup Heavy cream
- 1/4 cup Brewed espresso
- 1/4 cup Hazelnut liqueur (e.g., Frangelico)
- 1 Tbsp Unsalted butter
- 1/2 tsp Pure vanilla extract
- 1/4 tsp Sea salt
- Assorted dipping items such as strawberries, banana slices, marshmallows, pound cake cubes, and biscotti

Nutritional Information: Calories: 490, Protein: 3g, Carbohydrates: 35g, Fat: 35g, Fiber: 3g, Cholesterol: 40 mg, Sodium: 150 mg, Potassium: 200 mg

Directions:

1. The heavy cream and brewed espresso should be combined in a medium saucepan and heated to a gentle simmer.
2. Take off the heat and whisk in the chopped semi-sweet chocolate into the cream mixture. Allow to soften for one to two minutes.
3. Gently stir the chocolate mixture until smooth and fully incorporated.
4. Stir in the hazelnut liqueur, unsalted butter, vanilla extract, and sea salt, continuing to mix until the fondue is smooth and glossy.
5. Transfer the fondue mixture to your fondue pot and set it over the flame to keep warm.
6. Arrange the assorted dipping items on a platter around the fondue pot.
7. Using fondue forks or skewers, dip the items into the Hazelnut Espresso Fondue, coating them in the velvety chocolate.
8. Enjoy the burst of flavors as the fondue enriches each bite.

Tropical Coconut Chocolate Fondue

 4 SERVINGS 10 MINUTES 5 MINUTES

Indulge in an exotic escape with this Tropical Coconut Chocolate Fondue. A creamy and dreamy blend of rich chocolate and tropical coconut flavors, this fondue is like dipping your favorite fruits and treats into a sweet, island-infused paradise. It's a warm way to bring the tropics to your table any time of year, and it's perfect for sharing with friends and loved ones.

Equipment: Fondue pot, Heatproof mixing bowl (if melting chocolate via double boiler method), Fondue forks

Ingredients:

- 200g High-quality dark chocolate, broken into small pieces
- 1 cup Coconut cream
- 2 tbsp Coconut rum (optional)
- 1/2 tsp Pure vanilla extract
- Pinch of salt
- Assorted dippables: sliced bananas, pineapple chunks, mango pieces, strawberries, marshmallows, and pound cake cubes

Nutritional Information: Calories: 460, Protein: 4g, Carbohydrates: 28g, Fat: 36g, Fiber: 5g, Cholesterol: 2 mg, Sodium: 20 mg, Potassium: 322 mg

Directions:

1. Melt the dark chocolate and coconut cream together in a fondue pot or over a saucepan of simmering water in a heatproof mixing bowl over the stovetop (double boiler method). Stirring continuously, heat the mixture until the chocolate has melted completely and the mixture becomes smooth.
2. Add the pure vanilla essence, coconut rum, and a little teaspoon of salt, and whisk until thoroughly combined, if using.
3. If you are not using a fondue pot already, carefully move the bowl to the fondue stand once the sauce is smooth and well blended.
4. Arrange your selected fruits, marshmallows, and cake on a platter around the fondue pot.
5. Spear your desired dippables with a fondue fork and swirl them into the chocolate mixture, ensuring they are generously coated.
6. Enjoy the Tropical Coconut Chocolate Fondue while it's warm and velvety.

Toasted Almond and Amaretto Fondue

 6 SERVINGS 15 MINUTES 10 MINUTES

Indulge in the rich comfort of toasted almonds blended with the sweet, aromatic kick of amaretto, all swirled into a silky chocolate fondue. Perfect for a cozy night in or a gathering with friends, this recipe merges the classic charm of fondue with a sophisticated almond twist.

Equipment: Fondue pot, Heat-resistant spatula, Fondue forks or skewers

Ingredients:

- 12 oz Semi-sweet chocolate, chopped or chips
- 1 cup Heavy cream
- 1/2 cup Whole milk
- 2 tablespoons Amaretto liqueur
- 1/4 cup Toasted almonds, finely chopped
- A pinch of salt
- Assorted dippers such as strawberries, banana slices, marshmallows, biscotti, and pound cake cubes

Nutritional Information: Calories: 510, Protein: 5g, Carbohydrates: 40g, Fat: 36g, Fiber: 3g, Cholesterol: 55 mg, Sodium: 40 mg, Potassium: 210 mg

Directions:

1. Pour the heavy cream and milk into a medium saucepan and heat over medium heat until it starts to boil. Be vigilant not to let it come to a boil.
2. Reduce the heat to low and add the semi-sweet chocolate to the simmering cream mixture. Using a heat-resistant spatula, carefully stir the mixture until the chocolate is totally melted and smooth.
3. Stir in the amaretto liqueur, followed by the toasted almonds and pinch of salt. Continue to stir until everything is well combined and the fondue is smooth and glossy.
4. Transfer the chocolate mixture to your fondue pot set over a low flame to keep warm.
5. Serve with your choice of dippers, spearing them with fondue forks or skewers and swirling them in the decadent toasted almond and amaretto chocolate.

Bananas Foster Chocolate Fondue

 8 SERVINGS 15 MINUTES 10 MINUTES

Indulge in the intoxicating blend of creamy chocolate fondue and the caramelized charm of bananas foster. This dessert combines smooth chocolate with the flavors of ripe bananas, rum, and brown sugar for a sinfully delightful experience perfect for ending a meal on a high note or for a luxurious gathering.

Equipment: Fondue Pot, Small saucepan, Heatproof spatula

Ingredients:

- 8 oz Semi-sweet chocolate, chopped
- 2 medium Bananas, sliced
- 1/4 cup Dark rum
- 2 tbsp Unsalted butter
- 1/2 cup Brown sugar, packed
- 1 tsp Vanilla extract
- 1/4 tsp Ground cinnamon
- 1/2 cup Heavy cream

Nutritional Information: Calories: 340, Protein: 2g, Carbohydrates: 30g, Fat: 21g, Fiber: 2g, Cholesterol: 35 mg, Sodium: 25 mg, Potassium: 220 mg

Directions:

1. In a small pot over medium heat, melt butter. Add in the brown sugar, stirring until it's well combined and starts to melt.
2. Mix in the sliced bananas and cook for about 2 minutes until they are tender and coated in the caramel syrup.
3. Carefully pour in the dark rum and allow the mixture to cook for another minute. Optionally, flambe the rum by lighting it with a match to burn off the alcohol. Please do so with extreme caution.
4. Stir in the cinnamon and vanilla extract, cooking for an additional minute. Remove the bananas foster mixture from heat and set aside.
5. Heat the heavy cream in the fondue pot over low heat until it's heated but not boiling.
6. Gradually add in the chopped semi-sweet chocolate, continually stirring with the heatproof spatula until completely melted and smooth.
7. Once the chocolate is melted, gently fold in the bananas foster mixture until fully combined, keeping the fondue warm over low heat.
8. Serve immediately with an assortment of items for dipping, such as marshmallows, strawberries, pound cake cubes, and pretzel sticks.

Salted Caramel Pretzel Fondue

 6 SERVINGS 20 MINUTES 10 MINUTES

Dive into this sticky, sweet, and slightly salty decadence that combines the creamy complexities of caramel with the satisfying crunch of pretzels. This Salted Caramel Pretzel Fondue is perfect for those who adore a sweet and savory dessert experience.

Equipment: Fondue pot, Wooden skewers or fondue forks, Small saucepan

Ingredients:

- 8 ounces semisweet chocolate, coarsely chopped
- 1 cup caramel sauce
- 1/2 cup heavy cream
- One teaspoon sea salt plus additional for decoration
- 1 tablespoon unsalted butter
- Pretzels, for dipping
- Additional dippables of your choice (e.g., strawberries, marshmallows, apple slices, banana chunks, brownie bites)

Nutritional Information: Calories: 420, Protein: 3g, Carbohydrates: 46g, Fat: 24g, Fiber: 2g, Cholesterol: 35mg, Sodium: 587mg, Potassium: 202mg

Directions:

1. Warm the heavy cream in a small saucepan over medium heat until it's hot but not boiling, to start your fondue experience.
2. Add in the coarsely chopped semisweet chocolate to the saucepan, stirring continually until the chocolate has thoroughly melted into the cream, creating a smooth and velvety mixture.
3. Introduce the caramel sauce to the chocolate mixture, continuing to stir until the blend is homogeneous and exudes a rich, golden hue.
4. Stir the sea salt and butter into the chocolate-caramel mix until the butter is fully melted and the salt is evenly distributed, granting a perfect balance.
5. Transfer the luscious concoction into your preheated fondue pot, adjusting the heat to maintain a delicate simmer that encourages dipping without the threat of burning.
6. Skewer your chosen dippables such as pretzels, fruit pieces, or marshmallows, and dive into the fondue, twirling to coat with the thick, indulgent sauce.
7. When serving, add a light sprinkle of sea salt over the fondue-coated bite to elevate the sweet-savory contrast and enhance the overall flavor profile.

Black Forest Cake Fondue

 6 SERVINGS 15 MINUTES 5 MINUTES

Dive into the sumptuous flavors of a Black Forest Cake transformed into a lusciously velvety fondue. A harmony of rich chocolate, tart cherries, and a whisper of kirsch make this a dessert to remember. Perfect for dipping your favorite fruits, cake cubes, or marshmallows for an indulgent twist on traditional fondue.

Equipment: Fondue pot, Heat-resistant spatula, Measuring cups and spoons

Ingredients:

- 8 oz semi-sweet chocolate, finely chopped
- 1/2 cup heavy cream
- 1/4 cup cherry liqueur (kirsch)
- 1/2 cup canned cherries, drained and chopped
- 1 tsp vanilla extract
- A pinch of salt
- Fresh cherries, cake cubes, and marshmallows for dipping

Nutritional Information: Calories: 340, Protein: 2g, Carbohydrates: 28g, Fat: 22g, Fiber: 2g, Cholesterol: 35 mg, Sodium: 20 mg, Potassium: 220 mg

Directions:

1. Begin by placing the finely chopped semi-sweet chocolate into your fondue pot.
2. Heat the chocolate in a small saucepan over medium heat until it begins to simmer, then pour the heavy cream over the chocolate. Allow the chocolate to soften for a few minutes.
3. Cream and chocolate should be gently whisked together until the mixture is cohesive and creamy.
4. Stir in the cherry liqueur, chopped canned cherries, vanilla extract, and a pinch of salt, mixing until all the ingredients are well incorporated.
5. Set your fondue pot to a low setting to keep the chocolate warm and inviting.
6. Serve the Black Forest Cake Fondue with fresh cherries, bite-sized cubes of chocolate or vanilla cake, and marshmallows for a full experience.

Peanut Butter Cup Fondue

 4 SERVINGS   10 MINUTES   5 MINUTES

Immerse yourself in the creamy, dreamy union of rich chocolate and smooth peanut butter, all melded into a warm fondue that offers a dip into decadence with each bite. Perfect for an indulgent evening, this Peanut Butter Cup Fondue is a true crowd-pleaser, encapsulating the beloved flavors of classic peanut butter cups in a luscious, dippable form.

Equipment: Fondue pot, Heat-resistant rubber spatula, Fondue forks or skewers

Ingredients:
- 8 oz semi-sweet chocolate, chopped or chips
- 1/2 cup heavy cream
- 1/3 cup smooth peanut butter
- 1 tsp pure vanilla extract
- Pinch of salt
- Dippers such as strawberries, banana slices, marshmallows, pretzels, and pound cake cubes

Nutritional Information: Calories: 563, Protein: 8g, Carbohydrates: 38g, Fat: 42g, Fiber: 3g, Cholesterol: 41 mg, Sodium: 151 mg, Potassium: 221 mg

Directions:
1. Begin by preparing all your dippers. Wash and cut fruit if necessary, and slice the pound cake into bite-sized cubes. Place them so they can be easily accessed around the fondue pot on a dish.
2. Pour the heavy cream into the fondue pot and warm it over a low heat until it starts to simmer. Keep an eye on it to ensure it does not come to a boil.
3. Stirring continually with the rubber spatula until the chocolate melts completely and the mixture becomes smooth, gradually add the semi-sweet chocolate to the simmering cream.
4. Stir in the smooth peanut butter to the chocolate-cream mixture, and keep stirring until the peanut butter is thoroughly combined and the mixture is velvety.
5. Add the vanilla extract and a pinch of salt, stirring well to ensure all the flavors are melded.
6. Once the fondue is smooth and fully combined, it's ready to serve. Use the fondue forks or skewers to dip your chosen treats into the fondue, coating them in the peanut butter chocolate mixture.

Marshmallow S'mores Fondue

 4 SERVINGS   15 MINUTES   10 MINUTES

Savor the comforting tastes of a classic campfire recipe with a fondue twist. Our Marshmallow S'mores Fondue blends creamy chocolate with gooey marshmallows and a touch of coffee essence, perfect for dipping your favorite s'mores accompaniments. It's a crowd-pleasing dessert that invites everyone to gather around the pot for a communal, cozy, and utterly delightful experience.

Equipment: Fondue pot, Fondue forks, Heatproof bowl (if melting chocolate separately), Saucepan (if melting chocolate separately)

Ingredients:
- 8 oz Semisweet chocolate, chopped
- 1/2 cup Heavy cream
- 1/4 cup Brewed coffee, strong and at room temperature
- 1/2 cup Marshmallow creme
- 1 tsp Pure vanilla extract
- Pinch of salt
- Graham crackers, for dipping
- Marshmallows, for dipping
- Fresh strawberries, for dipping (optional)

Nutritional Information: Calories: 370, Protein: 3g, Carbohydrates: 38g, Fat: 22g, Fiber: 3g, Cholesterol: 30 mg, Sodium: 95 mg, Potassium: 270 mg

Directions:
1. In a fondue pot over low heat, warm the heavy cream and coffee together until hot but not boiling. If you don't have a fondue pot, heat the ingredients in a saucepan and then transfer to a heatproof serving bowl.
2. When the chocolate has melted and the mixture is smooth, gradually add the chopped chocolate to the liquid while stirring continuously.
3. Stir in the marshmallow creme, vanilla extract, and a pinch of salt, and continue to heat the mixture until everything is fully incorporated and warm, ensuring that it's kept warm without getting too hot to prevent scorching.
4. Once the fondue is smooth and fully combined, use the fondue forks to dip graham crackers, marshmallows, and strawberries into the chocolate mixture.
5. Enjoy the fondue while it's warm and the chocolate is still melty.

Irish Cream Chocolate Fondue

 6 SERVINGS 15 MINUTES 5 MINUTES

Dive into the indulgent world of Irish Cream Chocolate Fondue, where the rich flavors of premium chocolate and the warming embrace of Irish cream liqueur come together in a blend that's perfectly suited for any special occasion or a cozy night in. This chocolate fondue with an Irish twist is a sure way to delight your taste buds and excite your guests with a touch of elegance and a hint of spirited charm.

Equipment: Fondue Pot, Fondue Forks, Heat-Proof Bowl, Saucepan

Ingredients:

- 8 oz Dark Chocolate, finely chopped
- 1/2 cup Heavy Cream
- 1/3 cup Irish Cream Liqueur
- 2 tbsp Unsalted Butter
- 1 tsp Pure Vanilla Extract
- A pinch of Sea Salt

Nutritional Information: Calories: 350, Protein: 3g, Carbohydrates: 25g, Fat: 25g, Fiber: 3g, Cholesterol: 45 mg, Sodium: 35 mg, Potassium: 200 mg

Directions:

1. Begin by preparing your fondue station: set up the fondue pot on its stand and ensure your fondue forks are within easy reach for your guests.
2. Pour the heavy cream into the heat-proof bowl and place over a saucepan of simmering water to create a double boiler, making sure the bottom of the bowl doesn't touch the water.
3. Toss in the chopped dark chocolate and add it to the bowl of cream. To carefully stir the mixture until the chocolate melts and it becomes smooth, use a wooden spoon or silicone spatula.
4. Once combined, stir in the Irish Cream Liqueur, continuing to stir until it is fully incorporated into the chocolate mixture.
5. Remove the mixture from the heat. Add the vanilla essence, unsalted butter, and a little teaspoon of sea salt, stirring to incorporate everything thoroughly and give the fondue a glossy appearance.
6. Transfer the chocolate fondue to your preheated fondue pot, setting it to a low flame to keep the fondue warm and silky.
7. Serve immediately with an assortment of dippables such as strawberries, banana slices, marshmallows, pound cake cubes, or pretzels.

Chocolate Orange Liqueur Fondue

 6 SERVINGS 10 MINUTES 10 MINUTES

Whether it's date night or a gathering with friends, this Chocolate Orange Liqueur Fondue is a showstopper. Delight in the rich, smooth chocolate elegantly paired with the zesty allure of orange liqueur, offering a sophisticated twist to the classic chocolate fondue. Perfect as a dessert course or as the centerpiece of a dessert party!

Equipment: Fondue pot, Heat-resistant stirring spoon, Fondue forks or long skewers

Ingredients:

- 200 g (7 oz) High-quality dark chocolate
- 200 ml (7 oz) Heavy cream
- 50 ml (1.7 oz) Orange liqueur (such as Grand Marnier or Cointreau)
- Zest of 1 orange
- A pinch of salt
- 1 tsp Vanilla extract

Nutritional Information: Calories: 330, Protein: 2.9g, Carbohydrates: 20g, Fat: 25g, Fiber: 3g, Cholesterol: 45 mg, Sodium: 40 mg, Potassium: 250 mg

Directions:

1. Begin by breaking the dark chocolate into smaller pieces or chopping it to ensure it will melt evenly.
2. Heat the heavy cream in the fondue pot over a low flame until it starts to steam, being careful not to let it boil.
3. Add the chocolate chunks to the cream gradually while swirling constantly until the chocolate has melted and the liquid is smooth.
4. To blend the flavors, add the orange liqueur and whisk again for a minute more.
5. Add the freshly grated orange zest and a pinch of salt, then mix these into the fondue to infuse it with a subtle citrus aroma and balance the sweetness.
6. Mix in the vanilla extract, giving your fondue a final stir to ensure all the ingredients are well-integrated and the mixture is silky.
7. With the fondue now ready, keep the pot over a very subtle heat source to maintain its liquid state. Invite everyone to dip their preferred snacks using the fondue forks or skewers.

Mocha Java Chocolate Fondue

 6 SERVINGS   15 MINUTES   10 MINUTES

Indulge in the rich and aromatic blend of fine coffee and luxurious chocolate with the Mocha Java Chocolate Fondue. This sumptuous dessert will encapsulate the senses with its velvety texture and the deep, robust flavors of coffee-infused chocolate, elevating the traditional fondue experience to an irresistible coffee lover's dream.

Equipment: Fondue pot, Heatproof Stirring Spoon, Fondue Forks

Ingredients:

- 8 oz Semisweet Chocolate, chopped
- 1/2 cup Heavy Cream
- 1/4 cup Strong Brewed Coffee (preferably Java)
- 1 tsp Pure Vanilla Extract
- 2 Tbsp Coffee Liqueur (optional)
- Pinch of Salt
- Assorted Dippers (strawberries, marshmallows, biscotti, banana slices, etc.)

Nutritional Information: Calories: 348, Protein: 3g, Carbohydrates: 22g, Fat: 28g, Fiber: 2g, Cholesterol: 36 mg, Sodium: 38 mg, Potassium: 172 mg

Directions:

1. Begin by brewing a strong cup of Java coffee, allowing it to reach a robust flavor profile.
2. Combine the chopped semisweet chocolate and heavy cream in the fondue pot over low heat. Once the chocolate has melted completely and the mixture is smooth, carefully stir the mixture.
3. Gradually pour in the brewed coffee, stirring continuously to incorporate it fully into the chocolate mixture, creating a smooth mocha blend.
4. Stir in the pure vanilla extract, coffee liqueur if using, and a pinch of salt to enhance the flavors. Continue to cook the fondue for an additional 2-3 minutes on low heat, stirring occasionally to ensure it doesn't burn or stick to the bottom.
5. Once the fondue is smooth and all ingredients are well combined, arrange the dippers around the fondue pot on serving plates.
6. Spear the dippers using fondue forks and swirl them into the warm Mocha Java Chocolate Fondue to coat generously.
7. Serve immediately while the fondue is warm and enjoy the luxurious merger of chocolate and coffee flavors.

Red Velvet Cake Fondue

 6 SERVINGS   10 MINUTES   5 MINUTES

Dive into the luscious and indulgent world of red velvet in liquid form with this sumptuous Red Velvet Cake Fondue. Featuring the classic flavors of cocoa, buttermilk, and a touch of food coloring to achieve that iconic hue, this fondue is perfect for drizzling over pieces of pound cake, fresh strawberries, or marshmallows. It's a romantic and whimsical dessert that evokes the spirit of your favorite red velvet cake but with a fun, interactive twist.

Equipment: Fondue pot, Whisk, Heatproof spatula

Ingredients:

- 8 oz Semisweet chocolate, chopped
- 1/2 cup Heavy cream
- 1/4 cup Buttermilk
- 1 tbsp Unsweetened cocoa powder
- 2 tsp Red food coloring
- 1 tsp Vanilla extract
- Pinch of salt
- Cake and fruit for dipping

Nutritional Information: Calories: 292, Protein: 3g, Carbohydrates: 23g, Fat: 21g, Fiber: 2g, Cholesterol: 27 mg, Sodium: 18 mg, Potassium: 164 mg

Directions:

1. Combine the heavy cream, buttermilk, and cocoa powder in a medium-sized heatproof bowl. Stir thoroughly to completely incorporate the chocolate powder.
2. To make a double boiler, place the bowl over a saucepan of simmering water, being careful that the water does not contact the bottom of the bowl. Heat the liquid, stirring occasionally, until the cocoa is completely dissolved and it becomes warm.
3. When the chocolate has melted and the mixture is smooth, add the chopped semisweet chocolate to the bowl and stir constantly.
4. Add the vanilla essence, pinch of salt, and red food coloring; whisk until coloring is completely incorporated and the fondue has a consistent red velvet color.
5. Carefully transfer the red velvet chocolate mixture to your fondue pot and set it to a low heat to keep the fondue warm and smooth for dipping.
6. Serve with bite-sized pieces of pound cake, fresh strawberries, banana slices, marshmallows, or other dippable treats as desired.

Mint Chocolate Chip Fondue

 4 SERVINGS 10 MINUTES 5 MINUTES

Indulge in the refreshing essence of mint combined with rich, velvety chocolate in this Mint Chocolate Chip Fondue. This delicious twist on a classic dessert is perfect for those who crave the cool tingle of mint paired with the indulgent taste of creamy chocolate chips.

Equipment: Fondue pot, Heat-resistant spatula, Fondue forks or skewers

Ingredients:

- 8 oz Semisweet chocolate, chopped
- 3/4 cup Heavy cream
- 1 tbsp Unsalted butter
- 2 tsp Peppermint extract
- 1/3 cup Miniature chocolate chips
- Fresh mint leaves (optional, for garnish)

Nutritional Information: Calories: 410, Protein: 3g, Carbohydrates: 30g, Fat: 33g, Fiber: 2g, Cholesterol: 35 mg, Sodium: 25 mg, Potassium: 200 mg

Directions:

1. Place the chopped semisweet chocolate in the fondue pot.
2. In a small saucepan, heat the heavy cream over medium heat until it just starts to simmer. Be cautious not to let it boil over.
3. To soften the chocolate, pour the warm cream over it in the fondue pot and let it sit for one to two minutes. Add the tablespoon of unsalted butter.
4. Once the chocolate has completely melted and the mixture is smooth, carefully stir it with the heat-resistant spatula.
5. Add the peppermint extract to the chocolate mixture and stir well to incorporate, ensuring the fondue has a consistent minty flavor throughout.
6. Mix in the miniature chocolate chips, reserving a few to sprinkle on top for texture and aesthetics.
7. If using a traditional fondue set, light the fondue burner according to your fondue set's instructions to keep the chocolate warm for dipping.
8. Place the fondue pot on the table and provide guests with fondue forks or skewers to dip their favorite accompaniments such as strawberries, marshmallows, cubes of pound cake, or biscotti.
9. Garnish with fresh mint leaves and the reserved miniature chocolate chips just before serving.

Tiramisu Chocolate Fondue

 6 SERVINGS 10 MINUTES 10 MINUTES

Indulge in the rich and creamy flavors of Tiramisu Chocolate Fondue, a whimsical twist on the classic Italian dessert. This recipe combines the comfort of velvety chocolate with the robust notes of coffee, harmonized with a hint of liqueur, to create an unforgettable fondue experience perfect for dipping strawberries, ladyfingers, or marshmallows.

Equipment: Fondue pot, Heat-resistant spatula, Fondue forks or skewers

Ingredients:

- 8 oz Semi-sweet chocolate, chopped
- 1/2 cup Heavy cream
- 1/4 cup strong coffee or espresso, brewed
- 2 tbsp Mascarpone cheese
- 2 tbsp Coffee liqueur (e.g. Kahlúa), optional
- 1 tsp Vanilla extract
- 1/4 tsp Sea salt, fine
- Cocoa powder, for dusting
- For Dipping: Ladyfingers; Fresh strawberries, halved; Banana slices; Marshmallows; Pound cake, cubed

Nutritional Information: Calories: 320, Protein: 3g, Carbohydrates: 25g, Fat: 24g, Fiber: 2g, Cholesterol: 22 mg, Sodium: 90 mg, Potassium: 172 mg

Directions:

1. Add the chopped chocolate and heavy cream to the fondue pot; gently heat over low flame, stirring constantly with the spatula until the chocolate is melted and smooth.
2. Stir the brewed espresso (or strong coffee), mascarpone cheese, and coffee liqueur (if using) into the chocolate mixture until fully combined and the mixture is creamy.
3. Stir thoroughly to ensure that all of the flavors are evenly distributed after adding the sea salt and vanilla essence..
4. If needed, adjust the flame to keep the fondue warm but not hot, to avoid scorching.
5. Transfer the fondue pot to your serving table and light the fondue burner underneath to maintain the chocolate mixture's warmth.
6. Dust the top with a light sprinkling of cocoa powder for a touch of elegant bitterness that complements the sweet and creamy fondue.
7. Serve immediately with ladyfingers, strawberries, banana slices, marshmallows, and cubed pound cake for dipping.

Pomegranate Pistachio Chocolate Fondue

 4 SERVINGS   15 MINUTES   10 MINUTES

Dive into the luxurious combination of rich, dark chocolate elegantly enhanced with the tangy sweetness of pomegranate and the crunchy, nutty flavors of pistachio. This decadent fondue is a perfect balance of flavors and textures that will turn your dessert into a memorable affair.

Equipment: Fondue pot, Heatproof bowl, Stovetop

Ingredients:

- 8 ounces Dark chocolate, finely chopped
- 1/2 cup Heavy cream
- 1/4 cup Pomegranate juice
- 1 tablespoon Orange liqueur (optional)
- 1/2 cup Pomegranate seeds
- 1/4 cup Pistachios, shelled and chopped
- Pinch of Salt
- Assorted dippers such as strawberries, marshmallows, shortbread cookies, or pieces of pound cake

Nutritional Information: Calories: 380, Protein: 4g, Carbohydrates: 34g, Fat: 24g, Fiber: 5g, Cholesterol: 30 mg, Sodium: 85 mg, Potassium: 300 mg

Directions:

1. Prepare all dippers by slicing any large fruits and arranging them alongside marshmallows, cookies, and cake on a serving platter.
2. Melt the dark chocolate in a heatproof bowl over a pot of simmering water, being careful not to let the bowl touch the water, and stir occasionally until smooth.
3. The pomegranate juice and heavy cream should be brought to a simmer in a small saucepan over medium heat. Do not let it boil. Remove from heat.
4. Gradually mix the warm cream and pomegranate juice into the melted chocolate, stirring gently until the mixture is smooth. If using, stir in the orange liqueur.
5. Once fully combined, stir in half the pomegranate seeds and half the chopped pistachios, saving the rest for garnish.
6. Pour the chocolate mixture into the fondue pot and place it over low heat. Sprinkle with the remaining pomegranate seeds and pistachios on top just before serving.
7. Spear the dippers with fondue forks or skewers, dip into the chocolate mixture, and enjoy.

Honey Lavender Chocolate Fondue

 4 SERVINGS   15 MINUTES   10 MINUTES

Indulge in the floral notes of lavender and the natural sweetness of honey as they marry elegantly with rich melted chocolate in this Honey Lavender Chocolate Fondue. Perfect for a romantic evening or as a luxurious treat for your guests, this recipe transforms the traditional chocolate fondue into an innovative delight that tantalizes the senses.

Equipment: Fondue pot, Small saucepan, Wooden skewers or fondue forks

Ingredients:

- 200g high-quality dark chocolate, roughly chopped
- 100ml heavy cream
- 3 tbsp honey
- 1 tsp dried culinary lavender, plus extra for garnish
- A pinch of sea salt
- Assorted dippers: strawberries, sliced bananas, marshmallows, pound cake cubes, pretzels

Nutritional Information: Calories: 545, Protein: 6g, Carbohydrates: 49g, Fat: 37g, Fiber: 5g, Cholesterol: 31 mg, Sodium: 46 mg, Potassium: 522 mg

Directions:

1. In a small saucepan, lightly toast the dried lavender over low heat for about 1 to 2 minutes or until fragrant. Be attentive not to burn them.
2. Toss in the toasted lavender in a skillet with heavy cream. Stirring occasionally, slowly heat the mixture over low heat for three to five minutes. This will allow the lavender flavor to infuse into the cream.
3. Strain the cream through a fine sieve to extract the lavender. After adding the infused cream back to the saucepan, remove the solids.
4. Over low heat, add the chopped dark chocolate to the infused cream. Stir regularly until the chocolate has melted completely and the liquid is smooth.
5. Once all the ingredients are properly combined and the fondue takes on a glossy appearance, stir in the honey and a little teaspoon of sea salt.
6. Transfer the chocolate mixture to your fondue pot set on a low flame to keep warm. If your fondue pot doesn't have a heat source, serve immediately to prevent the fondue from solidifying.
7. Arrange your chosen dippers on a platter around the fondue pot.
8. Spear the dippers with wooden skewers or fondue forks, dip into the Honey Lavender Chocolate Fondue, and enjoy!

Chai Spice Chocolate Fondue

 4 SERVINGS 10 MINUTES 10 MINUTES

This Chai Spice Chocolate Fondue infuses the rich and creamy depths of dark chocolate with the warming spices found in Chai tea, creating an exotic and comforting dessert experience. Perfect for dipping fresh fruits, marshmallows, or chunks of pound cake, it's a unique twist on a classic fondue that will enchant your palate and take your guests on a flavorful journey.

Equipment: Fondue Pot, Small Saucepan, Whisk

Ingredients:

- 8 oz High-quality dark chocolate, chopped
- 1 cup Heavy cream
- 1 tsp Ground cinnamon
- 1/2 tsp Ground ginger
- 1/4 tsp Ground cloves
- 1/4 tsp Cardamom
- 1/4 tsp Nutmeg
- 1 pinch Black pepper
- 1/2 tsp Vanilla extract

Nutritional Information: Calories: 435, Protein: 3.8g, Carbohydrates: 26g, Fat: 36g, Fiber: 3g, Cholesterol: 68 mg, Sodium: 22 mg, Potassium: 340 mg

Directions:

1. Begin by preparing your dippers. Wash and cut fruits as needed and portion your marshmallows and pound cake cubes into accessible dishes.
2. The heavy cream should be slowly heated over low heat in the small saucepan until it starts to simmer. Take care to prevent it from boiling over.
3. Add in the cinnamon, ginger, cloves, cardamom, nutmeg, and a pinch of black pepper to the simmering cream, stirring the mixture thoroughly.
4. Gradually whisk in the chopped dark chocolate until the mixture is smooth and fully combined.
5. Stir in the vanilla extract, infusing the fondue with a depth of flavor.
6. Transfer the chocolate mixture into the fondue pot, making sure it stays heated by lighting it.
7. Arrange the dippers around the fondue pot and serve immediately. Use fondue forks or skewers to dip your chosen treats into the Chai Spice Chocolate Fondue.

Rocky Road Chocolate Fondue

 6 SERVINGS 15 MINUTES 10 MINUTES

Dive into the indulgent world of Rocky Road in a lusciously melted form with our Rocky Road Chocolate Fondue. Featuring the classic blend of rich chocolate, fluffy marshmallows, and crunchy nuts, this concoction is a fun and interactive dessert that will satisfy all your sweet tooth cravings. It's perfect for sharing with friends and family, making any gathering a memorable one.

Equipment: Fondue pot, Heat-resistant spatula, Fondue forks or skewers

Ingredients:

- 8 oz Semisweet chocolate, chopped
- 1/2 cup Heavy cream
- 1/4 cup Brewed coffee, cooled
- 1 tsp Vanilla extract
- 1/2 cup Mini marshmallows
- 1/2 cup Almonds, roasted and roughly chopped
- 1/4 cup Walnuts, roasted and roughly chopped

Nutritional Information: Calories: 382, Protein: 5g, Carbohydrates: 25g, Fat: 30g, Fiber: 3g, Cholesterol: 31mg, Sodium: 22mg, Potassium: 234mg

Directions:

1. In a medium saucepan over medium heat, bring the heavy cream to a simmer. Be careful not to let it boil. Remove from heat.
2. Add the chopped semisweet chocolate to the saucepan, letting it sit for a few minutes to gently melt from the heat of the cream.
3. Using a heat-resistant spatula, stir the chocolate and cream mixture until it becomes smooth and velvety.
4. Stir in the cooled brewed coffee and vanilla extract until fully incorporated. The coffee will deepen the chocolate flavor profiles and add a subtle richness.
5. Transfer the chocolate mixture to your fondue pot and keep the pot at a low heat to keep the fondue warm.
6. Gently fold in the marshmallows, almonds, and walnuts, being careful not to crush the marshmallows.
7. Serve immediately with fondue forks or skewers for dipping your favorite Rocky Road companions: chunks of brownie, pieces of graham crackers, or fresh fruit like strawberries and bananas.

Fig and Port Wine Chocolate Fondue

 6 SERVINGS   15 MINUTES   10 MINUTES

Indulge in the rich and elegant flavors of dried figs simmered in port wine, blended into a velvety dark chocolate fondue. The subtle sweetness and unique texture of the figs enhance the depth of the chocolate, making for a luxurious dessert perfect for any special occasion.

Equipment: Fondue pot, Small saucepan, Whisk, Cutting board, Knife

Ingredients:

- 8 oz High-quality dark chocolate, finely chopped
- 1 cup Heavy cream
- 1/2 cup Port wine
- 1/2 cup Dried figs, finely chopped
- 1 tbsp Honey
- 1/4 tsp Ground cinnamon
- A pinch of salt
- Assorted fondue dippers such as strawberries, banana slices, marshmallows, shortbread cookies, and pound cake cubes

Nutritional Information: Calories: 380, Protein: 3g, Carbohydrates: 33g, Fat: 25g, Fiber: 4g, Cholesterol: 35 mg, Sodium: 20 mg, Potassium: 340 mg

Directions:

1. Combine the port wine and honey in a small saucepan. Gently heat over medium-low flame until the honey dissolves completely.
2. Add the finely chopped dried figs to the saucepan and simmer for about 5 minutes, allowing the figs to soften and the mixture to thicken slightly.
3. While the figs simmer, heat the heavy cream in your fondue pot until it starts to steam but not boil.
4. Gradually whisk in the finely chopped dark chocolate into the hot cream until fully melted and smooth.
5. Add a small teaspoon of salt and the cinnamon, to taste.
6. Fold the port wine and fig mixture into the chocolate until uniformly combined.
7. Place the fondue pot over the burner set to low heat to keep the fondue warm.
8. Serve with an assortment of fondue dippers on the side.

Matcha White Chocolate Fondue

 4 SERVINGS   10 MINUTES   5 MINUTES

Indulge in the serene sweetness of matcha paired with rich, creamy white chocolate in this Matcha White Chocolate Fondue. It's a velvety concoction with a subtle grassy note that makes for an elegant dessert. Perfect for fruit dipping or pouring over cakes, this fondue melds the distinct flavors of East and West for a transcendent treat.

Equipment: Fondue pot, Heatproof bowl, Forks or fondue skewers

Ingredients:

- 200g High-quality white chocolate, chopped
- 100ml Heavy cream
- 1 Tbsp Matcha powder
- 2 Tbsp Unsalted butter
- 1 Tsp Pure vanilla extract
- A pinch of Salt
- Optional for dipping: Fresh strawberries, cubed pound cake, marshmallows, banana slices or other fondue dippables

Nutritional Information: Calories: 390, Protein: 4g, Carbohydrates: 25g, Fat: 31g, Fiber: 0g, Cholesterol: 35mg, Sodium: 55mg, Potassium: 167mg.

Directions:

1. Prepare your fondue skewers or forks and set aside with your chosen dippables.
2. To make a double boiler, add approximately one inch of water to a saucepan and set a heatproof bowl on top, making that the bowl stays above the water. Heat the water to a gentle simmer.
3. Once the butter has melted and the mixture is heated but not boiling, add the heavy cream and butter to the bowl.
4. Sift the matcha powder into the hot cream mixture to prevent lumps and whisk until fully blended.
5. When the chocolate has melted and the mixture is smooth, gradually add the chopped white chocolate to the mixture while stirring continuously.
6. Add a small amount of salt and the vanilla extract, tasting as you go.
7. Pour the smooth fondue into a fondue pot set over a gentle flame to keep warm.
8. Serve the fondue with your selection of dippables, using the skewers or forks to dip the items into the matcha white chocolate mixture.

Innovative Fondue Creations

Savory Pumpkin and Sage Cheese Fondue

 4 SERVINGS   20 MINUTES   10 MINUTES

Dive into autumnal bliss with this savory pumpkin and sage cheese fondue. The earthy tones of pumpkin puree blend harmoniously with the aromatic sage, while the richness of melted cheese creates a luxurious texture perfect for dipping your favorite breads and vegetables.

Equipment: Fondue pot, Whisk, Saucepan

Ingredients:

- 1 cup pumpkin puree
- 1.5 cups shredded Gruyère cheese
- 1 cup shredded Emmental cheese
- 2 tbsp cornstarch
- 1 cup dry white wine
- 1 garlic clove, minced
- 1 tbsp fresh sage, finely chopped
- 1/2 tsp nutmeg
- Salt and pepper to taste
- Crusty bread, apples, and broccoli for dipping

Nutritional Information: Calories: 450, Protein: 28g, Carbohydrates: 15g, Fat: 25g, Fiber: 2g, Cholesterol: 85 mg, Sodium: 620 mg, Potassium: 300 mg

Directions:

1. In a bowl, toss Gruyère and Emmental cheese with cornstarch until evenly coated. This step will help thicken the fondue and prevent the cheese from clumping.
2. Stir in the white wine and minced garlic, then place the saucepan over medium heat and gently simmer. Avoid letting it boil to ensure the alcohol cooks off without reducing too much of the liquid.
3. Stirring constantly, gradually add the cheese mixture to the pot. Stir in a figure-eight pattern to encourage even melting.
4. After the cheese has melted and become smooth, thoroughly mix in the pumpkin puree.
5. Mix in the chopped sage, nutmeg, and season with salt and pepper to taste. Keep stirring until everything is hot and well combined.
6. Pour the fondue into the preheated fondue pot and keep it warm over the flame.
7. Serve immediately with pieces of crusty bread, sliced apples, and lightly steamed broccoli for dipping.

Charred Jalapeño and Tequila Cheese Fondue

 4 SERVINGS   15 MINUTES   10 MINUTES

Exuberant with a smoky twist complemented by the sharp depth of tequila, this Charred Jalapeño and Tequila Cheese Fondue offers a tantalizing intersection of flavors that's sure to ignite your taste buds. An innovative fusion that transforms the classic fondue into a formidable foray into gourmet territory.

Equipment: Fondue pot, Chopping board, Knife, Measuring cups and spoons

Ingredients:

- 1 tablespoon Unsalted butter
- 1/4 cup White onion, finely chopped
- 2 Jalapeños, charred, seeds removed, and finely diced
- 3 tablespoons Silver tequila
- 1 clove Garlic, minced
- 1 cup Chicken broth
- 8 oz Gruyère cheese, shredded
- 8 oz Sharp cheddar cheese, shredded
- 2 tablespoons Cornstarch
- Fresh ground pepper, to taste
- Salt, to taste

Nutritional Information: Calories: 450, Protein: 28g, Carbohydrates: 6g, Fat: 33g, Fiber: 1g, Cholesterol: 100 mg, Sodium: 620 mg, Potassium: 80 mg

Directions:

1. Melt the butter in a fondue pot over a medium heat. Add the chopped onions and sauté for 2 to 3 minutes, or until transparent.
2. Stir in the charred diced jalapeños and minced garlic, sautéing for another minute until aromatic.
3. Carefully pour in the tequila, allowing the alcohol to cook off for about 2 minutes, then reduce the heat to low.
4. Gradually add the chicken broth into the mixture. Bring the mixture to a light simmer.
5. In a separate bowl, toss the shredded Gruyère and cheddar with cornstarch to coat.
6. Slowly add the cheeses to the fondue pot, stirring constantly in a figure-eight pattern to ensure even melting and prevent clumping.
7. After melting and becoming smooth, add salt and freshly ground pepper to taste.
8. Serve right away with your preferred dippers, including prepared meats, veggies, or crusty bread.

Matcha Green Tea Dessert Fondue

 4 SERVINGS　　 10 MINUTES　　 5 MINUTES

Delight in the harmony of East meets West with this Matcha Green Tea Dessert Fondue. The grassy notes of quality matcha powder blend with the luxurious creaminess of white chocolate, offering an elegant dipping experience. This innovative fondue is a perfect conversation starter, guaranteed to impress and satisfy the taste buds of green tea enthusiasts and dessert lovers alike.

Equipment: Fondue pot, Heatproof bowl, Whisk

Ingredients:

- 8 oz White Chocolate, finely chopped
- 1 cup Heavy Cream
- 2 tbsp Matcha Green Tea Powder
- 2 tbsp Unsalted Butter
- 1 tbsp Honey or to taste
- Assorted dippers (such as fresh fruit, pound cake, marshmallows, and biscotti)

Nutritional Information: Calories: 490, Protein: 4g, Carbohydrates: 35g, Fat: 38g, Fiber: 0g, Cholesterol: 120 mg, Sodium: 55 mg, Potassium: 160 mg

Directions:

1. Spoon the white chocolate into a medium-sized, heat-resistant bowl and reserve.
2. Pour the heavy cream into a small saucepan and boil over medium heat until it starts to simmer. Do not let it boil.
3. Add the matcha green tea powder and whisk until the powder is completely dissolved and the mixture is the same color.
4. Pour the hot matcha cream over the white chocolate, letting it sit for one minute to soften the chocolate.
5. When the chocolate has melted completely and the fondue is smooth, add the butter and honey and stir the mixture. If necessary, gently heat the bowl over a pot of simmering water to help the chocolate melt.
6. Transfer the smooth matcha mixture to your fondue pot and set it over the fondue burner to keep warm. Adjust the flame to maintain a gentle heat.
7. Serve with your choice of dippers arranged on a platter around the fondue pot.

Roasted Beet and Goat Cheese Fondue

 4 SERVINGS　　 15 MINUTES　　 45 MINUTES

This fondue remixes the traditional concept by introducing the earthy flavors of roasted beet melted into a smooth, tangy goat cheese base. A hint of espresso gives it a subtle coffee twist, making it a sophisticated choice for those who appreciate the melding of savory notes with the richness of coffee.

Equipment: Fondue pot, Blender, Oven, Baking sheet, Aluminum foil

Ingredients:

- 2 medium-sized red beets
- 10 oz soft goat cheese
- 1/2 cup heavy cream
- Two tablespoons of freshly made strong coffee or espresso
- 1 tsp cornstarch
- 1/2 tsp salt
- 1/4 tsp black pepper
- 1/4 tsp dried thyme
- Assorted dippers such as crusty bread, blanched vegetables, or apple slices

Nutritional Information: Calories: 380, Protein: 22g, Carbohydrates: 13g, Fat: 28g, Fiber: 3g, Cholesterol: 75 mg, Sodium: 560 mg, Potassium: 284 mg

Directions:

1. Set oven temperature to 400ºF, or 200ºC. Cut off the tops of the beets, cover each one with a piece of aluminum foil, and arrange on a baking pan. Roast for 45 minutes or until soft in the oven. When finished, remove the wrap and let it cool before slicing and peeling.
2. Puree the roasted beets in a blender until smooth.
3. Beat the cornstarch and heavy cream together in a bowl until no lumps remain.
4. Pour the heavy cream mixture into the fondue pot over medium heat. When the goat cheese has melted and the mixture is smooth, add it to the pot and stir constantly.
5. Stir in the pureed beets, espresso, salt, pepper, and dried thyme. Continue to cook, stirring until all ingredients are fully incorporated and the fondue is heated through.
6. Reduce the heat to low (or transfer to a fondue candle if not using an electric pot) to keep the fondue warm while serving.
7. Serve with your choice of dippers. Crusty bread, blanched vegetables, and apple slices complement the flavor profile nicely.

Smoked Salmon and Dill Fondue

 4 SERVINGS   15 MINUTES   10 MINUTES

This silky and luxurious fondue combines the rich flavors of smoked salmon with the aromatic freshness of dill. It's a sumptuous twist on classic fondue, offering a delectable blend of seafood zest and creamy fondue indulgence. This Smoked Salmon and Dill Fondue is ideal for a classy dinner party or a relaxing night in. It will serve as the focal point of a memorable culinary adventure.

Equipment: Fondue pot, Whisk, Saucepan

Ingredients:

- 200g Smoked Salmon, finely chopped
- One and a half cups of dry white wine, like Sauvignon Blanc
- 1 Garlic Clove, halved
- 2 1/2 cups Gruyère Cheese, grated
- 1/2 cup Cream Cheese
- 2 tbsp Fresh Dill, chopped
- 1 tbsp Lemon Juice
- 1 tsp Dijon Mustard
- 2 tsp Cornstarch
- Freshly Ground Black Pepper, to taste
- For Dipping: Cubed crusty bread, blanched asparagus, steamed baby potatoes, and/or crisp apple slices

Nutritional Information: Calories: 420, Protein: 23g, Carbohydrates: 6g, Fat: 31g, Fiber: 0g, Cholesterol: 105 mg, Sodium: 800 mg, Potassium: 200 mg

Directions:

1. To give a gentle garlic taste to the fondue pot, rub the interior with the halved garlic clove.
2. In a saucepan, heat the white wine over medium heat until hot, but not boiling.
3. Gradually add the Gruyère cheese to the wine, stirring continuously until the cheese is melted and the mixture is smooth.
4. In a small bowl, blend the cornstarch with a few tablespoons of the wine mixture to create a smooth paste, then whisk this back into the cheese mixture to thicken the fondue.
5. Add the cream cheese, stirring well until the mixture is uniformly smooth.
6. Stir in the chopped smoked salmon, fresh dill, lemon juice, and Dijon mustard. Continue to cook gently for a few minutes until everything is well combined and heated through.
7. Add freshly ground black pepper to taste when seasoning.
8. Transfer the fondue mixture to the prepared fondue pot set over its burner. Adjust the flame to maintain the fondue's warmth without letting it boil.
9. Serve with an array of dippable items, such as cubes of crusty bread, blanched asparagus, steamed baby potatoes, and crisp apple slices.

Dark Chocolate and Merlot Fondue

 4 SERVINGS   10 MINUTES   5 MINUTES

Indulge in the rich symphony of dark chocolate with the robust notes of a good Merlot. This fondue melds the complex flavors of a full-bodied wine with the velvety smoothness of bittersweet chocolate, creating a luscious dip that's perfect for an elegant evening in. Pure decadence in every spoonful, it pairs wonderfully with fruits and pastries.

Equipment: Fondue pot, Heat-resistant spatula, Fondue forks

Ingredients:

- 8 ounces high-quality dark chocolate (70% cacao), chopped
- 1/2 cup heavy cream
- 1/4 cup Merlot wine
- One tablespoon of sugar (optional, according on chocolate sweetness)
- 1/2 teaspoon pure vanilla extract
- A pinch of sea salt
- Fresh fruit (strawberries, banana slices, and apple chunks), for dipping
- Assorted pastries (pound cake cubes, brownie bites, marshmallows), for dipping

Nutritional Information: Calories: 440, Protein: 4g, Carbohydrates: 35g, Fat: 30g, Fiber: 5g, Cholesterol: 31 mg, Sodium: 41 mg, Potassium: 410 mg

Directions:

1. Heat the heavy cream in a medium saucepan over low heat until it starts to steam, being careful not to let it boil.
2. Add the chopped chocolate to the pot and give it a gentle stir with a spatula until the dark chocolate has completely melted into the cream and the mixture is smooth.
3. Pour in the Merlot wine, and if using, sprinkle in the sugar. Stir gently to combine until the fondue is smooth and uniform in texture.
4. Mix in the vanilla extract and a pinch of sea salt to enhance the chocolate and wine flavors.
5. Transfer the chocolate mixture into the fondue pot set over a low flame to keep it warm and smooth.
6. Arrange the fresh fruit and pastries on a platter around the fondue pot.
7. Use fondue forks to dip the fruits and pastries into the dark chocolate Merlot mixture, swirling each piece to coat it evenly.

Butternut Squash and Gorgonzola Fondue

  20 MINUTES 30 MINUTES

Savor the combination of gorgonzola and butternut squash, which is mixed into a rich and creamy fondue. This innovative twist on the classic Swiss dish introduces autumnal flavors complemented by the tangy intensity of gorgonzola, perfect for enveloping bread, vegetables, or apples for a cozy, fireside feast.

Equipment: Medium Saucepan, Stirring Spoon, Fondue Pot (optional)

Ingredients:

- 2 cups Peeled and diced butternut squash
- 1 tbsp Olive oil
- 1/2 tsp Salt
- 1/4 tsp Nutmeg, freshly grated
- 1 cup Dry white wine
- 1 Garlic clove, halved
- 8 oz Gorgonzola cheese, crumbled
- 2 tsp Cornstarch
- 1 tbsp Water
- Freshly ground black pepper, to taste
- Assorted dippers: Crusty bread cubes, apple slices, or blanched vegetables

Nutritional Information: Calories: 280, Protein: 12g, Carbohydrates: 15g, Fat: 18g, Fiber: 1g, Cholesterol: 40 mg, Sodium: 850 mg, Potassium: 224 mg

Directions:

1. Set oven temperature to 400°F, or 200°C. Add the nutmeg, salt, and olive oil to the cubed butternut squash. Place onto a baking sheet, then roast for 20 minutes, or until soft and beginning to turn golden.
2. Once the squash is roasted, blend it with 1/2 cup of white wine until smooth using a food processor or blender.
3. Rub the inside of a medium saucepan with the halved garlic clove, then discard the garlic.
4. Transfer the leftover half cup of white wine into the saucepan and place it on medium heat, allowing it to boil.
5. Stir the gorgonzola cheese into the wine gradually while stirring all the time until the cheese melts and the mixture becomes smooth. Avoid boiling.
6. In a small bowl, whisk together the cornstarch and water to create a slurry. Stir this into the cheese mixture.
7. Add the blended butternut squash to the cheese mixture and stir until fully incorporated and heated through.
8. Add freshly ground black pepper to taste while seasoning the fondue.
9. Serve the fondue with your preferred dippers after transferring it to a fondue pot that is placed over a flame to stay warm, if one is available.

Lemon Basil White Wine Seafood Fondue

 4 SERVINGS 20 MINUTES 15 MINUTES

Embark on an aromatic adventure with this bright and herbaceous seafood fondue. The marriage of tangy lemon, fragrant basil, and crisp white wine creates a zesty bath fit for the freshest of the ocean's bounty. Perfect for an intimate dinner or an elegant party appetizer, this fondue is sure to tantalize the senses and delight the palate.

Equipment: Fondue Pot, Stove, Mixing Bowl

Ingredients:

- A single cup of dry white wine, such Sauvignon Blanc
- 1 clove Garlic, minced
- 1 tbsp Cornstarch
- 1 tbsp Water
- 1 Lemon, zest and juice
- 1/4 cup Fresh Basil, finely chopped
- 1 lb Mixed Seafood (shrimp, scallops, and firm white fish), cut into bite-sized pieces
- Freshly Ground Black Pepper, to taste
- Salt, to taste
- Assorted vegetables (such as cherry tomatoes, artichoke hearts, and bell peppers) for dipping

Nutritional Information: Calories: 185, Protein: 25g, Carbohydrates: 5g, Fat: 1.5g, Fiber: 0.7g, Cholesterol: 180 mg, Sodium: 240 mg, Potassium: 300 mg

Directions:

1. In a mixing bowl, create a slurry by combining the cornstarch and water until smooth. Set aside.
2. Rub the inside of the fondue pot with the garlic clove to impart a mild garlic flavor, then discard the garlic.
3. Pour the white wine into the fondue pot and heat over medium flame until it simmers gently.
4. Stir the slurry once more and then add it to the wine while continuously stirring to thicken the mixture.
5. Add the lemon zest, lemon juice, and half of the chopped basil to the fondue pot, mixing well.
6. Allow the mixture to come back to a gentle simmer, then season with salt and pepper.
7. Reduce the heat to low and add the seafood to the fondue pot. Cook for 2-3 minutes or until the seafood is cooked through, being careful not to overcook.
8. Before serving, sprinkle the remaining basil on top for a fresh garnish.
9. Serve your Lemon Basil White Wine Seafood Fondue with an array of fresh vegetables for a delightful dipping experience.

Espresso Martini Chocolate Fondue

 6 SERVINGS 15 MINUTES 10 MINUTES

Indulge in the sophisticated fusion of a cocktail classic with the timeless appeal of chocolate fondue. This Espresso Martini Chocolate Fondue marries the rich, intense flavors of espresso and vodka with the silky smoothness of melting chocolate, creating an adult indulgence that will energize your dinner parties and delight your taste buds.

Equipment: Fondue pot, Small saucepan, Whisk, Fondue forks or skewers

Ingredients:

- 8 oz Semi-sweet chocolate chips or chunks
- 1/2 cup Heavy cream
- 1/4 cup Espresso or strong-brewed coffee, cooled
- 2 tbsp Coffee-flavored liqueur (like Kahlúa)
- 1 tbsp Vodka
- Pinch of sea salt

Nutritional Information: Calories: 310, Protein: 3g, Carbohydrates: 26g, Fat: 18g, Fiber: 2g, Cholesterol: 20 mg, Sodium: 35 mg, Potassium: 150 mg

Directions:

1. Heat the heavy cream in a small saucepan over medium heat until it starts to steam, taking care not to let it boil.
2. Place the chocolate chips in the fondue pot and pour the warm cream over them, allowing it to sit for about one minute to soften the chocolate.
3. Gently whisk the chocolate and cream together until the mixture is smooth and well combined.
4. Stir in the cooled espresso or coffee, coffee-flavored liqueur, vodka, and pinch of sea salt, mixing until the fondue is smooth and all ingredients are fully incorporated.
5. Set the fondue pot over its flame to keep the fondue at a consistent, dip-able temperature.
6. Serve immediately with a platter of your chosen dippers.

Sweet and Spicy Mango Habanero Fondue

 4 SERVINGS 20 MINUTES 10 MINUTES

Experience an exotic and tantalizing twist on classic fondue with this Sweet and Spicy Mango Habanero blend. Indulge in the lush sweetness of ripe mangoes perfectly complemented by the fiery kick of habanero – a delectable delight for those who crave a bold adventure in their dessert course.

Equipment: Fondue pot, Stove, Mixing bowls

Ingredients:

- 1 cup Mango puree
- 1/2 cup Heavy cream
- 100g White chocolate, chopped
- One habanero pepper, seeded and cut finely
- 2 tbsp Honey
- 1 tsp Lemon juice
- 1 pinch Salt
- Assorted dippers (such as strawberries, apple slices, marshmallows, pound cake cubes, etc.)

Nutritional Information: Calories: 235, Protein: 1.5g, Carbohydrates: 28g, Fat: 14g, Fiber: 1g, Cholesterol: 41 mg, Sodium: 55 mg, Potassium: 168 mg

Directions:

1. Add the finely diced habanero pepper to the mango puree in a small bowl, then set aside to allow the flavors to mingle.
2. Pour the heavy cream into the fondue pot and set over medium heat, allowing it to gently simmer.
3. When the white chocolate has completely melted into the cream, add it to the pot with the chopped chocolate and whisk constantly.
4. Stir in the honey, lemon juice, and a pinch of salt into the melted chocolate mixture until well combined.
5. Carefully blend in the mango-habanero mixture into the fondue pot, stirring gently to avoid splashing.
6. Once the fondue is smooth and fully combined, reduce the heat to low and keep it warm.
7. Arrange your chosen dippers on a platter around the fondue pot and serve immediately.

Balsamic Fig and Blue Cheese Fondue

 4 SERVINGS 15 MINUTES 10 MINUTES

Savor the robust and flavorful tastes of our inventive Balsamic Fig and Blue Cheese Fondue, which combines creamy blue cheese, sweet figs, and tart balsamic vinegar. This decadent concoction is perfect for those seeking a unique twist on the classic cheese fondue, offering a harmonious blend of complex tastes that will elevate your fondue experience.

Equipment: Fondue pot, Wooden spoon, Small saucepan

Ingredients:

- 1/2 cup Balsamic vinegar
- 1/2 cup Water
- 8 Fresh figs, chopped or 1/2 cup dried figs, rehydrated and chopped
- 1 tsp Brown sugar
- 1 tsp Fresh thyme leaves
- 16 oz Blue cheese, crumbled
- 2 tbsp Cornstarch
- A quarter cup of sherry or dry white wine
- Freshly ground black pepper, to taste
- Crusty bread, vegetables, and apple slices for dipping

Nutritional Information: Calories: 565, Protein: 22g, Carbohydrates: 26g, Fat: 40g, Fiber: 3g, Cholesterol: 75 mg, Sodium: 1395 mg, Potassium: 300 mg

Directions:

1. Balsamic vinegar, water, figs, brown sugar, and thyme leaves should all be combined in a small saucepan. Simmer for around ten minutes over medium heat, or until the figs are soft and the balsamic reduces to a thicker consistency. Take off the heat and give it a little time to cool.
2. Toss the blue cheese crumbles with cornstarch in a bowl, ensuring they are evenly coated.
3. Over medium-low heat, start warming the blue cheese and cornstarch mixture in the fondue pot, stirring gently.
4. Gradually add the white wine or sherry to the fondue pot, stirring constantly. Continue heating and stirring once the cheese has melted and the mixture is smooth.
5. Once smooth, add the balsamic fig reduction into the cheese fondue mixture. Stir until all ingredients are well-incorporated.
6. Add freshly ground black pepper to taste with the fondue.
7. Serve warm with your choice of dippables such as crusty bread, fresh vegetables, or apple slices.

Thai Peanut and Coconut Curry Fondue

 4 SERVINGS 15 MINUTES 10 MINUTES

Taste the exotic aromas of Thailand with this fondue of peanut and coconut curry. This innovative fondue merges the creamy richness of coconut milk with the savory punch of peanut butter, elevated by a melody of Thai spices that will transport your taste buds to the streets of Bangkok. It's perfect for dipping an assortment of meats, vegetables, and crusty bread for a culinary adventure right at your dining table.

Equipment: Fondue pot, Stove, Whisk

Ingredients:

- 1 cup Coconut milk
- 1/2 cup Creamy peanut butter
- 2 tbsp Red curry paste
- 1 tbsp Brown sugar
- 2 tsp Soy sauce
- 1 tsp Lime juice
- 1/4 tsp Salt
- 1 clove Garlic, minced
- 1 tbsp Fresh ginger, grated
- 1/4 cup Fresh cilantro, chopped
- Two finely sliced green onions (optional) as a garnish
- Crushed peanuts for garnish (optional)

Nutritional Information: Calories: 305, Protein: 7g, Carbohydrates: 12g, Fat: 27g, Fiber: 2g, Cholesterol: 0 mg, Sodium: 480 mg, Potassium: 295 mg

Directions:

1. In a medium saucepan, combine the coconut milk, peanut butter, and red curry paste over medium heat. Stir continuously until the mixture is well-blended.
2. Fold in the brown sugar, soy sauce, lime juice, salt, garlic, and ginger into the mixture. Whisk the ingredients together until the sugar is all dissolved and the mixture is smooth.
3. After transferring the mixture to the fondue pot, adjust the temperature to ensure that it stays heated.
4. Just before serving, sprinkle the fresh cilantro into the fondue and give it one final gentle stir to distribute the herbs.
5. Garnish with green onions and crushed peanuts if desired, providing visual appeal and a satisfying crunch.

Whiskey and Cola Glazed Meat Fondue

 6 SERVINGS   15 MINUTES   10 MINUTES

Experience bold and tantalizing flavors with this Whiskey and Cola Glazed Meat Fondue. A perfect harmony of rich whiskey and sweet cola caramelized to a sticky glaze that will have your meats aspiring to new heights. Gather your friends for an unforgettable fondue party that combines the thrill of grilling with the fun of communal dining.

Equipment: Fondue pot, fork skewers or fondue forks, stove or portable burner

Ingredients:

- 1 cup Whiskey
- 1 cup Cola
- 2 tbsp Brown sugar
- 2 tbsp Soy sauce
- 1 tsp Garlic powder
- 1/2 tsp Black pepper, ground
- 2 lb Beef tenderloin, cut into bite-sized cubes (can also use chicken or pork)
- 2 tbsp Cornstarch (optional, for thickening)
- Assorted vegetables for dipping (such as bell peppers, mushrooms, and onion wedges)

Nutritional Information: Calories: 388, Protein: 24g, Carbohydrates: 10g, Fat: 12g, Fiber: 0g, Cholesterol: 80 mg, Sodium: 330 mg, Potassium: 356 mg

Directions:

1. In a medium saucepan, combine the whiskey, cola, brown sugar, soy sauce, garlic powder, and black pepper. Stir well to combine.
2. Slowly boil the mixture over medium-high heat. When the sauce has reduced by half and become slightly syrupy, decrease heat to medium-low and simmer for 8 to 10 minutes. For a thicker glaze, mix 2 tablespoons of cornstarch with a little water and add to the glaze, stirring until thickened.
3. While the glaze is simmering, prepare the fondue pot on the burner and preheat as per the manufacturer's instructions.
4. Skewer the cubes of meat onto fondue forks. Once the glaze is ready, pour it into the fondue pot.
5. Cook the meat in the Whiskey and Cola glaze by dipping and stirring for 2-3 minutes per piece, or until desired doneness is achieved. Vegetables can also be dipped and cooked in the glaze.
6. Enjoy the cooked meat and vegetables by placing them on a plate and allowing them to cool for a moment before eating.

Pesto and Parmesan Cheese Fondue

 4 SERVINGS   15 MINUTES   10 MINUTES

Experience the harmonious blend of Italian flavors with this Pesto and Parmesan Cheese Fondue. A delightful twist on the traditional fondue, this recipe marries the aromatic basil pesto with creamy Parmesan, creating a lusciously savory dipping experience that's perfect for entertaining or a special night in.

Equipment: Fondue pot, Mixing bowl, Whisk

Ingredients:

- 1 cup Dry white wine
- 1 clove Garlic, halved
- 2 cups Shredded Parmesan cheese
- 1 tbsp Cornstarch
- 1/4 cup Basil pesto
- Fresh ground pepper, to taste
- Optional dippers: Crusty bread cubes, grilled vegetables, boiled new potatoes, or roasted chicken pieces

Nutritional Information: Calories: 390, Protein: 21g, Carbohydrates: 4g, Fat: 31g, Fiber: 0g, Cholesterol: 44 mg, Sodium: 880 mg, Potassium: 60 mg

Directions:

1. After giving the fondue pot a flavor boost by rubbing the garlic halves inside, throw the garlic away.
2. Transfer the dry white wine into the fondue pot and place it on medium heat, allowing it to boil slowly.
3. In a mixing bowl, toss the shredded Parmesan cheese with the cornstarch to coat. This helps thicken the fondue and prevents clumping.
4. Gradually add the Parmesan cheese to the wine, stirring continuously with the whisk until fully melted and the fondue mixture is smooth. Be careful not to let the fondue come to a boil.
5. Add the basil pesto and simmer for a few more minutes while stirring. Season with fresh ground pepper to taste.
6. Once the fondue is thick and smooth, reduce heat to very low to keep it warm. To keep anything from sticking at the bottom, stir from time to time.
7. Serve immediately with your choice of dippers—crusty bread cubes complement the pesto and Parmesan flavors perfectly.

Raspberry Chipotle Chocolate Fondue

 6 SERVINGS   15 MINUTES   10 MINUTES

Dive into the spicy and sweet flavors of this Raspberry Chipotle Chocolate Fondue, where the richness of chocolate meets the zing of raspberry and the smoky heat of chipotle for a daringly delicious treat. Perfect for those who love a kick of spice with their sweet.

Equipment: Fondue pot, Heat-resistant spatula, Fondue forks

Ingredients:

- 200g good-quality dark chocolate, roughly chopped
- 1 cup heavy cream
- 1/3 cup raspberry preserves
- 2 tablespoons brown sugar
- 1-2 teaspoons chipotle chili powder (adjust to taste)
- 1/2 teaspoon smoked paprika (optional for extra smokiness)
- Fresh raspberries for garnish
- Assorted dippers: strawberries, marshmallows, brownie bites, pretzels, biscotti

Nutritional Information: Calories: 380, Protein: 3g, Carbohydrates: 30g, Fat: 28g, Fiber: 3g, Cholesterol: 54 mg, Sodium: 26 mg, Potassium: 201 mg

Directions:

1. The heavy cream should be heated slowly over medium heat in a small saucepan so that it is heated but not boiling.
2. Slowly whisk in the brown sugar until dissolved.
3. Gradually add the chopped dark chocolate to the saucepan, stirring continuously until the chocolate is completely melted and the mixture is smooth.
4. Add the smoked paprika (if using), chipotle chile powder, and raspberry preserves. Stir until all the ingredients are fully combined and the fondue is smooth.
5. When everything is well combined and cooked through, pour the chocolate fondue into the fondue pot and place it over a low fire to stay warm.
6. Arrange your chosen dippers on a platter alongside the fondue pot.
7. Garnish with fresh raspberries on top for a burst of color and extra flavor.
8. Serve with fondue forks, and enjoy immediately for best results.

Saffron and Seafood Bouillon Fondue

 4 SERVINGS   20 MINUTES   30 MINUTES

Dive into the opulence of the sea with this Saffron and Seafood Bouillon Fondue. It blends the luxurious saffron aroma with the fresh, briny flavors of premium seafood. Ideal for those who enjoy an elevated dining experience with an innovative twist.

Equipment: Fondue pot, Small saucepan, Chef's knife, Cutting board

Ingredients:

- 4 cups Fish or vegetable stock
- 1 pinch Saffron threads
- 12 oz Mixed seafood (shrimp, scallops, and firm white fish like halibut), cleaned and cut into bite-sized pieces
- 1/4 cup White wine
- 2 cloves Garlic, minced
- 1 Shallot, finely chopped
- 1 tsp Fresh lemon zest
- 1/2 tsp Sea salt
- 1/4 tsp White pepper
- 1 tbsp Fresh chives, chopped for garnish
- Assorted vegetables (such as blanched asparagus, carrots, or broccoli florets) for dipping
- Pieces of crusty bread for dipping

Nutritional Information: Calories: 200, Protein: 24g, Carbohydrates: 10g, Fat: 2g, Fiber: 1g, Cholesterol: 85 mg, Sodium: 700 mg, Potassium: 450 mg

Directions:

1. The fish or vegetable stock should be simmered over medium heat in a small pot. Add saffron threads and let them steep for 5 minutes, allowing the saffron to infuse the stock with its color and distinctive flavor.
2. In your fondue pot, gently warm the white wine, garlic, and shallot until fragrant – be careful not to let them brown.
3. Strain the saffron-infused stock into the fondue pot and discard the solids. Season the bouillon with lemon zest, sea salt, and white pepper.
4. Over the fondue burner, bring the mixture to a slow simmer. You want a light bubble – not boiling – to gently cook the seafood and vegetables.
5. Starting with the firmest fish pieces, guests can skewer their choice of seafood and vegetables, then dip and swirl it in the fondue to cook to their liking.
6. Once cooked, sprinkle with fresh chives and enjoy the delicate pieces of seafood and vegetables by dipping them in the fragrant saffron bouillon or with pieces of crusty bread that will soak up the delicious flavors.
7. Continue cooking and enjoying until all seafood and vegetables have been savored.

Apple Cider and Cheddar Cheese Fondue

 4 SERVINGS 10 MINUTES 15 MINUTES

Dive into the flavors of autumn with this unique Apple Cider and Cheddar Cheese Fondue. Combining the tart and sweet undertones of apple cider with the creamy, sharp taste of aged cheddar cheese, this innovative fondue will be a hit at any gathering. Whether it's a cozy night in or an elegant party, this fondue is a conversation starter.

Equipment: Fondue Pot, Whisk, Wooden Spoon

Ingredients:

- 1 cup Apple cider
- 1 tbsp Cornstarch
- 1/2 tsp Mustard powder
- 1/4 tsp Paprika
- 1/8 tsp Nutmeg, freshly grated
- 16 oz Aged Cheddar Cheese, shredded
- 1 Garlic clove, halved
- Salt and pepper to taste
- Assorted dippers (e.g., cubed bread, apples, broccoli, or pretzels)

Nutritional Information: Calories: 470, Protein: 28g, Carbohydrates: 15g, Fat: 33g, Fiber: 0g, Cholesterol: 100 mg, Sodium: 620 mg, Potassium: 103 mg

Directions:

1. In a small bowl, combine cornstarch, mustard powder, paprika, and nutmeg. Set aside.
2. Rub the inside of the fondue pot with the garlic halves to infuse it with flavor; then discard the garlic.
3. Fill the fondue pot with the apple cider and cook it gently over medium heat.
4. Gradually add the shredded cheddar cheese to the pot, stirring constantly with a whisk or wooden spoon to prevent any lumps from forming.
5. Sprinkle in the cornstarch mixture while continuously stirring to thicken the fondue.
6. Once all the cheese is melted and the fondue is smooth, adjust the seasoning with salt and pepper.
7. Reduce heat to low (or switch to fondue burner), and serve immediately with your choice of dippers.

Moroccan Harissa and Lamb Broth Fondue

 6 SERVINGS 30 MINUTES 120 MINUTES

Experience the flavors of Morocco with this distinctive and hearty fondue, featuring a spicy harissa and robust lamb broth base. Ideal for dipping an array of meats, vegetables, and bread, this recipe creates an adventurous culinary journey right at your dinner table.

Equipment: Fondue pot, Stove, Sharp Knife, Cutting board, Ladle

Ingredients:

- 1.5 lbs bone-in lamb shoulder, trimmed and cubed
- 2 tbsp olive oil
- 1 large yellow onion, chopped
- 4 garlic cloves, minced
- 1 tsp ground cumin
- 1 tsp smoked paprika
- 2 tbsp harissa paste, adjust to taste
- 6 cups chicken or beef stock
- Add freshly ground black pepper and salt to taste.
- Fresh cilantro leaves for garnish
- Dipping ingredients: cubed meats (such as beef, chicken), bell peppers, mushrooms, cherry tomatoes, and crusty bread

Nutritional Information: Calories: 342, Protein: 37g, Carbohydrates: 7g, Fat: 18g, Fiber: 1g, Cholesterol: 97 mg, Sodium: 703 mg, Potassium: 497 mg

Directions:

1. Heat the olive oil in a big pot over medium heat. Brown the lamb pieces until they are golden on all sides. Remove and set aside.
2. In the same pot, add more oil if necessary, and sauté the chopped onions until they are soft and translucent. Add the minced garlic, cumin, and smoked paprika, and cook until fragrant, for about 1 minute.
3. Stir in the harissa paste to combine, cooking for another minute to release its flavors.
4. Return the lamb to the pot and add the chicken or beef stock. Season with salt and pepper, then bring the broth to a simmer. Cover and cook on low heat for about 1.5-2 hours, or until the lamb is tender.
5. Skim off any foam that arises to ensure a clearer broth.
6. Once the lamb is tender, strain the broth to remove the solids, then return the clear broth to the pot.
7. Preheat your fondue pot while you bring the broth to a light simmer again.
8. Carefully transfer the hot broth to the fondue pot and set it to the appropriate temperature to maintain a gentle simmer.
9. Arrange your chosen dipping ingredients on platters around the fondue pot.
10. Skewer your chosen dippable items and immerse them into the broth until cooked to your preference. Garnish with fresh cilantro leaves.
11. Enjoy this spicy and aromatic Moroccan-inspired fondue!

Rose Water and Pistachio Dessert Fondue

 4 SERVINGS   15 MINUTES   10 MINUTES

Immerse yourself in the fragrant allure of the Middle East with this Rose Water and Pistachio Dessert Fondue. Each bite will transport you to a realm of exotic flavors, blending the subtle floral notes of rose with the crunchy, earthy undertones of pistachios. A delightful harmony of tastes that's perfect for an elegant wrap-up to any fine dining experience!

Equipment: Fondue pot, Heat source (candle or burner), Fondue forks

Ingredients:

- 200g White chocolate, chopped
- 150ml Heavy cream
- 2 tbsp Rose water
- 1/4 cup Pistachios, crushed
- Pinch of Salt
- Assorted fondue dippers such as strawberries, marshmallows, small pieces of cake, etc. (to serve with the fondue)

Directions:

1. The heavy cream and white chocolate should be combined in a medium-sized heatproof bowl.
2. Gently heat the mixture over a pot of simmering water, stirring constantly until the white chocolate is fully melted and the mixture is smooth.
3. Remove the bowl from heat and stir in the rose water and a pinch of salt.
4. Pour the mixture into the fondue pot set over your heat source to keep it warm and smooth.
5. Sprinkle the crushed pistachios over the top of the fondue, stirring slightly to mix in some while leaving the rest as a garnish on top.
6. Serve immediately with a platter of assorted dippers.

Nutritional Information: Calories: 412, Protein: 4g, Carbohydrates: 33g, Fat: 29g, Fiber: 1g, Cholesterol: 35 mg, Sodium: 87 mg, Potassium: 201 mg

Garam Masala Vegetable Broth Fondue

 6 SERVINGS   30 MINUTES   30 MINUTES

This velvety Garam Masala Vegetable Broth Fondue infuses the hearty flavors of India with the communal joy of fondue. Exotic garam masala spices blend with a wholesome vegetable broth, providing an aromatic base for dipping an assortment of fresh vegetables, tofu, and bread. It's a perfect way to gather friends and family for a fun and unique dining experience.

Equipment: Fondue pot, forks or skewers, cutting board, knife

Ingredients:

- 4 cups Vegetable broth
- 1 tbsp Garam masala
- 1 tsp Ground cumin
- 1 tsp Ground coriander
- 1/2 tsp Turmeric powder
- 1/2 tsp Chili powder (adjust to taste)
- 1 tbsp Cornstarch
- 1 tbsp Water
- Assorted vegetables (such as bell peppers, zucchini, and mushrooms), cubed
- Cubed firm tofu
- Cubed crusty bread
- Salt to taste
- Fresh cilantro, chopped for garnish

Directions:

1. In your fondue pot, combine 4 cups of vegetable broth, 1 tbsp of garam masala, 1 tsp of ground cumin, 1 tsp of ground coriander, 1/2 tsp of turmeric powder, and chili powder. Stir over medium heat until the spices are well mixed and the broth is fragrant.
2. Once the broth starts simmering, reduce the heat. In a small bowl, mix 1 tbsp of cornstarch with 1 tbsp of water to create a slurry. Stir the slurry into the broth to thicken it slightly. This will help the spices cling to the dipping ingredients.
3. Prepare your assorted vegetables by washing, cutting, and arranging them on a serving platter alongside cubed tofu and bread.
4. Once the broth is thickened and heated through, it's ready for dipping. Use fondue forks or skewers to dip the vegetables, tofu, and bread cubes into the hot spiced broth.
5. Cook each item until tender or heated through, usually about 30 seconds to 2 minutes, depending on the item's size and density.
6. Adjust the seasoning with salt if necessary and garnish the fondue with fresh chopped cilantro before serving.

Nutritional Information: Calories: 120, Protein: 6g, Carbohydrates: 18g, Fat: 2g, Fiber: 4g, Cholesterol: 0 mg, Sodium: 750 mg, Potassium: 360 mg

Bourbon Bacon Chocolate Fondue

 8 SERVINGS 15 MINUTES 10 MINUTES

Dive into the smoky and sweet symphony of flavors with our Bourbon Bacon Chocolate Fondue. Combining rich dark chocolate, the earthy essence of coffee, the warmth of bourbon, and the savory crunch of bacon, this fondue turns any gathering into an indulgent feast.

Equipment: Fondue pot, Wooden skewers or fondue forks, Small saucepan

Ingredients:

- 1 cup Heavy cream
- 8 oz Dark chocolate, chopped
- 1/2 cup Brewed coffee, strong
- 2 tbsp Bourbon
- 1/4 cup Brown sugar
- 1/2 tsp Sea salt
- 1/2 tsp Vanilla extract
- 6 slices Bacon, cooked crisp and crumbled

Nutritional Information: Calories: 420, Protein: 5g, Carbohydrates: 30g, Fat: 30g, Fiber: 2g, Cholesterol: 40 mg, Sodium: 260 mg, Potassium: 230 mg

Directions:

1. In a small saucepan, heat the heavy cream over medium heat until it begins to simmer.
2. Reduce the heat to low and add the chopped dark chocolate, stirring until completely melted and smooth.
3. Stir in the brewed coffee, bourbon, brown sugar, and sea salt, continuing to stir until the mixture is uniform.
4. Remove from heat and blend in the vanilla extract.
5. Transfer the mixture into your fondue pot and keep warm.
6. Sprinkle the crumbled bacon on top of the chocolate mixture or on a separate plate for guests to add to their skewers.
7. Serve with an array of dippings such as fresh strawberries, banana slices, marshmallows, and cake cubes.
8. Ensure the fondue remains warm for a soft dipping consistency, being careful not to overheat as it may cause the chocolate to seize.

Chimichurri Beef Broth Fondue

 4 SERVINGS 20 MINUTES 10 MINUTES

Dive into the bold flavors of South America with this Chimichurri Beef Broth Fondue. The traditional Argentinian chimichurri sauce infuses the broth with a tangy, herby zing, making it perfect for cooking succulent pieces of beef to dip into even more chimichurri sauce on the side. A carnivore's delight and a fresh take on classic fondue!

Equipment: Fondue pot, Forks or skewers, Saucepan

Ingredients:

- 4 cups Beef broth
- 8 oz Sirloin steak, cut into bite-sized cubes
- 1/2 cup Fresh parsley, finely chopped
- 1/4 cup Fresh cilantro, finely chopped
- 3 tbsp Red wine vinegar
- 4 Garlic cloves, minced
- 3/4 cup Olive oil
- 1 tbsp Oregano, dried
- 1 tsp Red pepper flakes
- Salt and pepper to taste

Nutritional Information: Calories: 475, Protein: 18g, Carbohydrates: 4g, Fat: 44g, Fiber: 1g, Cholesterol: 40 mg, Sodium: 420 mg, Potassium: 300 mg

Directions:

1. Begin by preparing the chimichurri sauce. In a bowl, combine parsley, cilantro, red wine vinegar, garlic, olive oil, oregano, red pepper flakes, salt, and pepper. Whisk together until well combined and set aside.
2. Pour the beef broth into the fondue pot and heat until it begins to simmer. Add 3 tablespoons of the chimichurri sauce you just prepared into the broth, stirring to infuse the flavors.
3. While the broth is heating, season the sirloin steak pieces with a bit of salt and pepper.
4. Once the broth is simmering, use fondue forks or skewers to dip the steak pieces into the broth, cooking them to your desired level of doneness.
5. Serve immediately, allowing guests to cook their steak pieces in the broth, and use the remaining chimichurri sauce as a dipping sauce.

Wasabi and Ginger Cheese Fondue

 4 SERVINGS 20 MINUTES 10 MINUTES

Ignite your palate with the zesty kick of wasabi and the sharp, aromatic twist of ginger in this bold cheese fondue. It's an unexpectedly delightful combination that offers a fusion of East meets West, perfect for those who desire to venture beyond traditional fondue flavors.

Equipment: Fondue pot, Small saucepan, Whisk

Ingredients:

- 200g Gruyère cheese, grated
- 200g Emmental cheese, grated
- 2 tsp cornstarch
- 1 cup dry white wine
- 1 tbsp lemon juice
- 1 clove of garlic, halved
- 1 tsp wasabi paste, or to taste
- 1 tbsp fresh ginger, finely grated
- Salt to taste
- Freshly ground pepper to taste
- A pinch of sugar
- Fresh dill or chives, chopped (for garnish)

Nutritional Information: Calories: 420, Protein: 28g, Carbohydrates: 4g, Fat: 32g, Fiber: <1g, Cholesterol: 95 mg, Sodium: 620 mg, Potassium: 120 mg

Directions:

1. In a bowl, combine the grated Gruyère and Emmental cheese with the cornstarch, tossing to coat evenly.
2. Rub the inside of the fondue pot with the halved garlic clove to infuse it with a hint of garlic.
3. Fill the fondue pot with the wine and lemon juice, then gradually simmer over medium heat—do not boil.
4. To keep the cheese from balling up, gradually add the cheese mixture to the saucepan while stirring continuously in a zigzag motion as opposed to a circular one.
5. Grated ginger and wasabi paste are added to the smooth, completely melted cheese. To adjust the wasabi to your desired level of heat, season with salt, pepper, and a small teaspoon of sugar.
6. Continue to cook for a few minutes until the fondue is thickened to your liking. If it's too thick, you can add a splash of wine to thin it out.
7. Transfer the fondue pot to its base over a gentle flame.
8. Garnish with chopped dill or chives for an added layer of flavor and a burst of color.

Salted Honey and Walnut Fondue

 4 SERVINGS 10 MINUTES 15 MINUTES

Indulge in the comforting embrace of this salted honey and walnut fondue, a delectable twist on the classic that blends the natural sweetness of honey with the rich, earthy crunch of walnuts, all harmoniously balanced with a hint of sea salt. This enchanting blend will be the star of any fondue party, offering a warm and inviting dip that pairs perfectly with an array of dippers such as fresh fruit, bread, or even marshmallows.

Equipment: Fondue pot, Stirring spoon, Chopping board, Knife

Ingredients:

- 1 cup Heavy cream
- 1/2 cup Honey
- 1 tsp Sea salt, finely ground
- 1 tbsp Unsalted butter
- 1 cup Walnuts, chopped and toasted
- 3 tbsp Cornstarch
- 2 tbsp Water

Nutritional Information: Calories: 440, Protein: 5g, Carbohydrates: 26g, Fat: 37g, Fiber: 1g, Cholesterol: 68 mg, Sodium: 588 mg, Potassium: 125 mg

Directions:

1. In a dry skillet over medium heat, toast the chopped walnuts until fragrant and beginning to brown. Remove from heat and set aside.
2. Combine the heavy cream, honey, and sea salt in the fondue pot. Stirring periodically, cook over medium heat until ingredients are well combined and mixture achieves a soft simmer.
3. In a small bowl, mix the cornstarch and water to create a slurry. Slowly add the cornstarch slurry to the fondue pot, stirring constantly to prevent lumps.
4. When the unsalted butter is added to the saucepan, toss it around until it melts completely and is mixed into the fondue.
5. Once the fondue mixture thickens, fold in the toasted walnuts, reserving a small amount for garnish.
6. Continue to cook for another 2-3 minutes, ensuring that the fondue has thickened to a desirable consistency and the flavors have melded together.
7. Remove from heat and transfer the fondue pot to its base to keep warm. Sprinkle the remaining toasted walnuts on top just before serving.

Roasted Garlic and Mushroom Broth Fondue

 4 SERVINGS 20 MINUTES 30 MINUTES

Dive into the earthy flavors of roasted garlic and mushrooms in this innovative broth fondue. The umami-rich combination creates a hearty experience that's perfect for dipping crusty bread, tender vegetables, or even your favorite meats. This broth fondue promises a cozy and aromatic adventure for the palate.

Equipment: Fondue pot, Stove, Roasting pan, Garlic press, Chef's knife, Cutting board

Ingredients:

- 1 head Garlic, roasted
- 2 cups Beef or vegetable broth
- 1 cup Baby Bella mushrooms, thinly sliced
- 1/2 cup Shiitake mushrooms, thinly sliced
- 1 tbsp Olive oil
- 1 tsp Fresh thyme leaves
- 1/2 tsp Salt
- 1/4 tsp Freshly ground black pepper
- Fresh parsley, finely chopped for garnish

Nutritional Information: Calories: 80, Protein: 3g, Carbohydrates: 8g, Fat: 4g, Fiber: 1g, Cholesterol: 0 mg, Sodium: 870 mg, Potassium: 210 mg

Directions:

1. Set oven temperature to 400°F, or 200°C. Slice the top of the garlic head off so the cloves are visible. Drizzle with olive oil, wrap in foil, and roast in the oven for 30 minutes, or until cloves are soft and caramelized.
2. Add the beef or vegetable broth to a fondue pot and heat it to a moderate simmer over medium heat.
3. For maximum taste, remove the roasted garlic cloves from their shells and smash them using a garlic press before adding them to the simmering stock.
4. Stir in the baby Bella and shiitake mushrooms and cook for about 5 minutes until they are tender and the broth is aromatic with the scent of garlic and mushrooms.
5. Stir together the salt, pepper, and fresh thyme leaves.
6. Reduce the heat so that it stays at a low simmer. It's time to serve the fondue.
7. Garnish with fresh parsley and serve with a platter of dippables such as crusty bread, blanched vegetables, or cooked meats.
8. Adjust the heat as necessary during the meal to keep the fondue at a steady simmer.

Maple and Pecan Dessert Fondue

 4 SERVINGS 15 MINUTES 10 MINUTES

Satisfy your sweet tooth with this ultimate twist on a classic fondue. The Maple and Pecan Dessert Fondue combines the rich, velvety taste of maple syrup with the nutty crunch of pecans, creating a decadent dipping experience perfect for fruits, cakes, or marshmallows. A hint of coffee adds a sophisticated depth, ensuring that each bite is as tantalizing as the last.

Equipment: Fondue pot, Wooden skewers or fondue forks, Saucepan

Ingredients:

- 1 cup Heavy cream
- 1/2 cup Pure maple syrup
- 1 tablespoon Instant coffee granules
- 6 ounces Dark chocolate, chopped
- 1 tablespoon Unsalted butter
- 1 teaspoon Vanilla extract
- 1/4 teaspoon Salt
- 3/4 cup Pecans, chopped and toasted
- Assorted dippers (such as fresh strawberries, sliced bananas, chunks of angel food cake, marshmallows, etc.)

Nutritional Information: Calories: 610, Protein: 6g, Carbohydrates: 50g, Fat: 46g, Fiber: 3g, Cholesterol: 60 mg, Sodium: 170 mg, Potassium: 350 mg

Directions:

1. The heavy cream and maple syrup should be heated in a saucepan over medium heat, without boiling.
2. Stir in the instant coffee granules until fully dissolved.
3. Once the chocolate has melted completely and the liquid is smooth, turn the heat down to low and stir in the chopped dark chocolate.
4. Remove from heat and stir in the butter, vanilla extract, and salt until well combined.
5. Transfer the mixture into the fondue pot set over a low flame to keep it warm.
6. Sprinkle the toasted chopped pecans on top just before serving.
7. Arrange your desired dippers on a platter around the fondue pot. Skewer the dippers with wooden skewers or fondue forks and enjoy dipping them into the maple and pecan fondue.

Spicy Kimchi and Cheddar Fondue

 4 SERVINGS 15 MINUTES 10 MINUTES

Infuse your fondue night with a tantalizing twist! This Spicy Kimchi and Cheddar Fondue offers a compelling fusion of creamy cheese melded with the bold flavors of traditional Korean kimchi. Its fiery kick and umami-rich taste make for a mouthwatering culinary adventure that's perfect for dipping bread, vegetables, or even meats.

Equipment: Fondue pot, Wooden spoon, Cutting board

Ingredients:

- 8 oz Sharp cheddar cheese, shredded
- 2 tbsp Cornstarch
- 1 cup Whole milk
- 1/2 cup Kimchi, chopped
- 2 tsp Kimchi juice, from the kimchi jar
- 1 Garlic clove, minced
- 1/2 tsp Korean red pepper flakes (gochugaru)
- 1/2 tsp Soy sauce
- Freshly ground black pepper, to taste
- Green onions, sliced (for garnish)

Nutritional Information: Calories: 356, Protein: 21g, Carbohydrates: 7g, Fat: 28g, Fiber: 0.5g, Cholesterol: 89 mg, Sodium: 512 mg, Potassium: 141 mg

Directions:

1. Toss the shredded cheddar cheese and cornstarch in a bowl until the cheese is well covered. By doing this, the fondue will get thicker and not clump.
2. In the fondue pot, slowly heat the whole milk over medium heat until it starts to boil. Steer clear of boiling.
3. Gradually add the cornstarch-coated cheddar to the pot, stirring gently with a wooden spoon until the cheese is completely melted and the mixture is smooth.
4. Stir in the chopped kimchi, kimchi juice, minced garlic, Korean red pepper flakes, and soy sauce, blending well.
5. Stirring often, cook for a further two to three minutes to allow the flavors to mingle and prevent the fondue from sticking to the bottom of the pot.
6. Add a dash of freshly ground black pepper for seasoning.
7. Once the fondue is smooth and all ingredients are well-incorporated, reduce the heat to low or warm setting (if your fondue pot has this option) to maintain the fondue's temperature.
8. Garnish with sliced green onions just before serving.

Prosecco and Strawberry Chocolate Fondue

 6 SERVINGS 15 MINUTES 10 MINUTES

Delight in the effervescent allure of Prosecco paired with the luscious notes of ripe strawberries and rich chocolate. This innovative fondue sets the stage for a magical dessert experience, perfect for celebrations or indulgent treats amidst friends and family.

Equipment: Fondue Pot, Heatproof Bowl, Saucepan

Ingredients:

- 8 oz High-quality Milk Chocolate, chopped
- 4 oz High-quality Dark Chocolate, chopped
- 1 cup Fresh Strawberries, pureed
- 1/2 cup Prosecco
- 1/4 cup Heavy Cream
- 2 tbsp Unsalted Butter
- Selection of Dippers: Fresh Strawberries, Sliced Bananas, Marshmallows, Pound Cake Cubes, Pretzels, Biscotti

Nutritional Information: Calories: 395, Protein: 4g, Carbohydrates: 45g, Fat: 22g, Fiber: 3g, Cholesterol: 18 mg, Sodium: 20 mg, Potassium: 234 mg

Directions:

1. In a heatproof bowl, mix the chopped milk and dark chocolate pieces.
2. Combine the strawberry puree, Prosecco, and heavy cream in a saucepan, and heat the mixture over medium heat until it starts to steam but not boil.
3. Pour the hot Prosecco-strawberry mixture over the chocolate and let it sit for 1-2 minutes to allow the chocolate to soften.
4. Once the chocolate has melted completely and the fondue is smooth, gently stir the mixture. Add the unsalted butter and continue to whisk until fully incorporated.
5. Transfer the chocolate fondue to the fondue pot and set it over a low flame to keep warm.
6. Serve with a selection of dippers such as fresh strawberries, sliced bananas, marshmallows, pound cake cubes, pretzels, and biscotti.

Black Garlic and Brie Cheese Fondue

 4 SERVINGS 15 MINUTES 10 MINUTES

Indulge in the deliciously unique combination of creamy brie and the sweet, umami depth of black garlic with this innovative fondue. Ideal for special occasions or a gourmet gathering, this fondue offers a luxurious twist on a traditional favorite, promising to enchant the palate of cheese connoisseurs and adventurous foodies alike.

Equipment: Fondue pot, Stovetop or portable burner, Fondue forks or skewers

Ingredients:

- 400 g Brie cheese, rind removed and cubed
- 1 cup Dry white wine
- 2 tbsp Cornstarch
- 3-4 cloves Black garlic, mashed into a paste
- 1/2 cup Milk
- 1 tbsp Lemon juice
- A pinch Nutmeg
- A pinch Salt
- Freshly ground black pepper, to taste
- Assorted dippers (e.g., bread cubes, steamed vegetables, apple slices, or roasted potatoes)

Nutritional Information: Calories: 497, Protein: 26g, Carbohydrates: 12g, Fat: 36g, Fiber: 0g, Cholesterol: 100 mg, Sodium: 758 mg, Potassium: 184 mg

Directions:

1. In a small bowl, combine cornstarch with lemon juice until well mixed. Set this slurry aside for later use.
2. Transfer the dry white wine into the fondue pot and warm it over a medium heat source without letting it boil.
3. Gradually add the cubed brie to the wine, stirring gently until the cheese begins to melt.
4. Incorporate the black garlic paste into the melting cheese. Continue to stir, ensuring the garlic is evenly distributed throughout the fondue.
5. Once the cheese has mostly melted, stir in the milk to create a smoother consistency.
6. Add the cornstarch slurry to the cheese mixture, stirring constantly as the fondue begins to thicken.
7. Season the fondue with nutmeg, salt, and freshly ground black pepper. Adjust these seasonings to taste.
8. Reduce the heat to low, allowing the fondue to gently simmer for a few minutes until it reaches desired thickness and creaminess.
9. Serve the fondue warm with your choice of dippers, using fondue forks or skewers.

Antipasto Italiano Cheese Fondue

 6 SERVINGS 20 MINUTES 10 MINUTES

Dive into the flavors of Italy with this Antipasto Italiano Cheese Fondue, a savory blend that melds the hearty and robust essence of antipasto with the creamy decadence of traditional fondue. A perfect centerpiece for any gathering, this fusion appeals to both cheese fondue connoisseurs and lovers of Italian cuisine.

Equipment: Fondue pot, Wooden spoons, Fondue forks

Ingredients:

- 8 oz Gruyère cheese, shredded
- 8 oz Fontina cheese, shredded
- 2 tbsp Cornstarch
- 1 cup Dry white wine
- 2 tbsp Garlic, minced
- Half a cup of sun-dried tomatoes in oil, emptied, then cut
- Sliced and pitted 1/4 cup of Kalamata olives
- 1/4 cup Fresh basil, chopped
- 1/4 cup Roasted bell peppers, chopped
- 1 tbsp Capers, drained
- 1 tsp Italian seasoning
- Salt and pepper to taste

Nutritional Information: Calories: 340, Protein: 22g, Carbohydrates: 8g, Fat: 24g, Fiber: 1g, Cholesterol: 90 mg, Sodium: 620 mg, Potassium: 150 mg

Directions:

1. In a large bowl, toss both Gruyère and Fontina cheese with cornstarch to coat evenly. Set aside.
2. In the fondue pot, over medium heat, bring the white wine to a gentle simmer.
3. Lower the heat and add the garlic, stirring until aromatic, about 1 minute.
4. Add the cheese mixture to the pot gradually while stirring continuously in a zigzag motion (to avoid the cheese from balling up) until the cheese is smooth and fully melted.
5. Stir in the sun-dried tomatoes, kalamata olives, basil, roasted bell peppers, and capers, and mix well.
6. Add salt, pepper, and Italian seasoning to taste, and stir until everything is well blended and heated through.
7. Turn down the heat. Serve right along with your preferred dippers, like grilled veggies, bits of crusty bread, or Italian cured meats.

Conclusion

As we wrap up our culinary journey with **"Ultimate Coffee Recipe Book: Over 150 Recipes to Master the Art of Fondue from Traditional to Innovative,"** it's clear that fondue is more than just food—it's a festive ritual that brings people together. This guide has equipped you with everything from classic recipes to innovative twists that reinvigorate this beloved tradition. Whether you're a seasoned chef or a curious newcomer, this book aims to transform how you view and enjoy fondue.

Celebrate the Diversity of Fondue

Each page of this book has been crafted to enrich your cooking and dining experience, offering over 150 ways to engage with fondue. From the creamy depths of traditional cheese fondues to the rich, decadent layers of chocolate fondue, and the robust flavors of broth and oil fondues, there's a recipe here to captivate any palate.

Why This Fondue Cookbook is Essential

"Fondue is perfect for any occasion," isn't just a saying—it's a promise. This book delivers on that promise by providing detailed, easy-to-follow instructions and tips that ensure fondue success at home. It's designed to inspire both novice cooks and culinary experts to explore the versatility and joy of fondue cooking.

Extend Your Fondue Repertoire

The recipes in "Ultimate Coffee Recipe Book" encourage culinary creativity and are perfect for any gathering. They transform simple ingredients into exquisite meals that foster warmth and connection among diners. With this book, your fondue pot becomes a vessel of endless possibilities, making every meal an occasion.

We Value Your Feedback

As you embark on your fondue-making adventures, we invite you to share your experiences. Your feedback is invaluable and helps others discover the joys of fondue. After delving into the recipes and tips provided in this book, please take a moment to leave a review on Amazon. Tell us about your favorite recipes, your fondue parties, and how this book has made a difference in your culinary pursuits.

Index

Mediterranean Seafood Saffron Broth 33
Mexican Fiesta Broth Fondue 39
Middle Eastern Sumac Broth Fondue 44
Midnight Dark Chocolate & Sea Salt Fondue 64
Mint Chocolate Chip Fondue 75
Mocha Java Chocolate Fondue 74
Moroccan Harissa and Lamb Broth Fondue 88
Moroccan Lemon & Olive Broth Fondue 35
Moroccan Spiced Carrot Fondue 59

N

Neuchâtel Nectar Fondue 23
New England Seafood Broth Fondue 40
Nordic Dill & Juniper Broth Fondue 40

O

Old Bay Seafood Fondue 56
Orange Zest and Grand Marnier Fondue 67
Orchard Blue Cheese Fondue 19

P

Pacific Rim Ginger Broth Fondue 36
Panko Crusted Mushroom Fondue 51
Parisian Nights Gruyère Fondue 16
Parmesan Asparagus Fondue 57
Peanut Butter Cup Fondue 72
Peppermint Patty Chocolate Fondue 68
Pesto and Parmesan Cheese Fondue 86
Pomegranate Pistachio Chocolate Fondue 76
Prosecco and Strawberry Chocolate Fondue 93
Provencal Herb de Provence Broth Fondue 41

R

Raspberry Chipotle Chocolate Fondue 87
Red Velvet Cake Fondue 74
Rich Caramel Milk Chocolate Fondue 65
Roasted Beet and Goat Cheese Fondue 81
Roasted Garlic and Mushroom Broth Fondue 92
Roasted Garlic and Thyme Fondue 30
Rocky Road Chocolate Fondue 77
Roman Holiday Mozzarella Fondue 20
Rose Water and Pistachio Dessert Fondue 89
Rosemary Lamb Kebab Fondue 54
Russian Dill & Mustard Broth Fondue 46
Rustic Raclette Fondue 24

S

Saffron Elegance Fondue 26
Saffron and Seafood Bouillon Fondue 87
Salted Caramel Pretzel Fondue 71
Salted Honey and Walnut Fondue 91
Savoie's Secret Fondue 17
Savory Garlic Chicken Broth Fondue 33
Savory Pumpkin and Sage Cheese Fondue 80
Savory Sausage & Pepper Fondue 51
Sea Salt and Vinegar Potato Fondue 55
Sichuan Spicy Tofu Fondue 60
Smoked Salmon and Dill Fondue 82
Smoky Bacon Chocolate Fondue 68
Smoky Mountains Fondue 19
Southern Fried Green Tomato Fondue 62
Spanish Chorizo & Paprika Broth Fondue 43
Spiced Wine and Swiss Fondue 28
Spicy Aztec Chocolate Fondue 66
Spicy Buffalo Cauliflower Fondue 52
Spicy Kimchi and Cheddar Fondue 93
Sweet and Sour Pork Fondue 54
Sweet and Spicy Mango Habanero Fondue 84
Swiss Bliss Emmental Fondue 22
Szechuan Spicy Broth Fondue 41

T

Tandoori Vegetable Skewer Fondue 56
Tex-Mex Queso Fundido Fondue 59
Thai Coconut Lemongrass Fondue 37
Thai Peanut and Coconut Curry Fondue 85
Tiramisu Chocolate Fondue 75
Toasted Almond and Amaretto Fondue 70
Tropical Coconut Chocolate Fondue 69
Truffled Fontina Velvet 27
Turkish Delight Broth Fondue 46
Tuscan Fontina Dream 17
Tuscan Tomato Basil Broth Fondue 34

V

Vietnamese Pho Broth Fondue 38

W

Wasabi and Ginger Cheese Fondue 91
Whiskey and Cola Glazed Meat Fondue 86
White Chocolate Raspberry Swirl Fondue 65

Z

Zesty Lemon Chicken Fondue 52

Made in the USA
Las Vegas, NV
10 December 2024

13760415R00057